SEEKING SPIRITUAL INTIMACY

Journeying Deeper with Medieval Women of Faith

GLENN E. MYERS

Foreword by JAMES M. HOUSTON

IVP Books

An imprint of InterVarsity Press
Downers Grove, Illinois

InterVarsity Press
P.O. Box 1400, Downers Grove, IL 60515-1426
World Wide Web: www.ivpress.com
E-mail: email@ivpress.com

InterVarsity Press® is the book-publishing division of InterVarsity Christian Fellowship/USA®, a movement of students and faculty active on campus at hundreds of universities, colleges and schools of nursing in the United States of America, and a member movement of the International Fellowship of Evangelical Students. For information about local and regional activities, write Public Relations Dept., InterVarsity Christian Fellowship/USA, 6400 Schroeder Rd., P.O. Box 7895, Madison, WI 53707-7895, or visit the IVCF website at <www.intervarsity.org>.

All Scripture quotations, unless otherwise indicated, are taken from the Holy Bible, New International Version®. NIV®. Copyright ©1973, 1978, 1984 by International Bible Society. Used by permission of Zondervan Publishing House. All rights reserved.

While all stories in this book are true, some names and identifying information in this book have been changed to protect the privacy of the individuals involved.

Excerpts from Mechthild of Magdeburg: The Flowing Light of the Godhead, *translated by Frank Tobin, Copyright ©1998 by Frank Tobin. Paulist Press, Inc., New York/Mahwah, NJ. Reprinted by permission of Paulist Pess, Inc. www.paulistpress.com*

Excerpts from Hadewijch: The Complete Works, *translated by Mother Columba Hart OSB, Copyright 1980 by The Missionary Society of St Paul the Apostle in the State of New York. Paulist Press, Inc., New York/Mahwah, NJ. Reprinted by permission of Paulist Press, Inc. www.paulistpress.com*

Design: Cindy Kiple
Interior design: Beth Hagenberg
Cover image: Lady in a white cap by Hans the Younger Holbein. National Trust/Art Resource, NY.
Interior photographs taken by the author.

ISBN 978-0-8308-3551-5

Printed in the United States of America ∞

Library of Congress Cataloging-in-Publication Data

Myers, Glenn E., 1958-
  Seeking spiritual intimacy: journeying deeper with medieval women
of faith / Glenn E. Myers.
      p. cm.
  Includes bibliographical references (p.   )
  ISBN 978-0-8308-3551-5 (pbk.: alk. paper)
  1. Beguines—Spiritual life. 2. Spiritual life—Christianity. I.
Title
  BX4272.M94 2011
  274'.04082—dc22

                                                    2010052965

P	18	17	16	15	14	13	12	11	10	9	8	7	6	5	4	3	2	1
Y	26	25	24	23	22	21	20	19	18	17	16	15	14	13	12	11		

Dedicated to my mother,

Beatrice,

and the godly women who have

always surrounded her

Contents

Foreword

ONE OF THE GREAT AFFIRMATIONS of the apostle Paul is in 2 Corinthians 5:16-17:

> For the love [*agape*] of Christ constrains us . . . that they who live should no longer live unto themselves but unto him who for their sakes died and rose again.

All that *agape* means, and all action that flows from *agape,* in fact proceeds only from God as expressed in Jesus Christ. The source, the motive, the expressions of this love—the fruits of its actions and relationships—are all of Christ's love for us. Likewise when Paul states, "I live by the faith of the Son of God" (Galatians 2:20), is he boasting of his trust in Christ, or rather is he acknowledging that he lives in the merit of the Son's relationship of trust with and in the Father?

It is the intense awareness of such love that captivated the remarkable women of the twelfth and thirteenth centuries detailed in this book—the "Beguines." Although not all understood theologically (as deeply as the apostle teaches) the substitutionary nature of the cross of Christ, love is not intended to be a subject of discourse and debate; it is to be *experienced* and *expressed.* It is the enjoyment of Christ's *agape* that inspired the Beguines to contribute a distinctive new way of life for the church. To reintroduce this way of life to Western evangelicals today is what Glenn Myers has dared to do!

This book is not a historical treatise about this remarkable Beguine movement. Nor is it a theological essay. Rather it is written as a devotional manual to challenge Christians today to fall in love with Christ and to grow in that love.

The author has historical, geographical and theological skills in reciting the lives and writings of the Beguines. But the simple, clear text of this work belies the depths of its subject matter. Some of the Beguines were highly educated; others were relatively simple. But taken together they have composed some of the most complex spiritual writings in the history of the church—much of which is still not fully understood.

Perhaps, in fact, this deep-simple idea—that Christ's *agape* is not to be dissected but embraced—explains why, seemingly throughout Christian history, there has been a rift between personal lovers of Christ and the officials of the institutional church. As again Paul states, "the love of Christ . . . passes knowledge" (Ephesians 3:19). Like the prophet Ezekiel, who had a vision of a river he could not cross, only swim in (Ezekiel 47:5), so we are invited to explore in a fresh way the love-consciousness of being indwelt by Christ, to serve Christ among all who need him.

The Flemish Beguines had a word for this love-consciousness: *minne*. One of the wisest of these women, Hadewijch, sees *minne* as the very meaning of the Christian existence:

The power which I come to know in the nature of *minne*
Throws my mind into bewilderment:
The thing has no form, no manner, no outward appearance.
Yet it is the substance of my joy . . .

Seeking Spiritual Intimacy is written in a new genre for most readers—adapting the lives and writings of the saintly women of the High Middle Ages and applying their experience of God's love in the domesticity of our own daily lives, to renew the love of Christians today. As on a pilgrimage, twelve stages are unfolded to us, with practical exercises to live out what we have been reading. Like stepping stones across the river of life, we are guided and guarded by a devout and skillful spiritual mentor in Glenn Myers. Such a resource is powerfully countercultural to our prevailing narcissistic society, reflected even in the church today. It challenges the shallowness of religious activism, and it gives renewed hope to Christians who seek a more uninhibited, passionate experience of Christ's love, who desire their identity to be more "Christlike." Perhaps like Dante in his *Commedia:*

> In the middle of my life I awoke in a dark wood where the true way was wholly lost. Alarmed I ask, "do I really know what it means to be a Christian?"

This may be the guidebook to set you on your way, content to have only one identity: a "lover of Christ."

James M. Houston

Introduction

Invitation to a Deeper Life

One thing I ask of the LORD,
    this is what I seek:
that I may dwell in the house of the LORD
    all the days of my life,
to gaze upon the beauty of the LORD
    and to seek him in his temple.

PSALM 27:4

You should always look fixedly on your Beloved whom you desire. For he who gazes on what he desires becomes ardently enkindled, so that his heart within him begins to beat slowly because of the sweet burden of love. And through perseverance in this holy life of contemplation, wherein he continually gazes on God, he is drawn within God. Love ever makes him taste [God's love] so sweetly that he forgets everything on earth.

HADEWIJCH OF BRABANT

OUR HEARTS LONG FOR FRESH SPRINGS of spiritual water. Inside we yearn for something more, something deeper. When we come to Christ our thirst does not end. Instead it intensifies. As we mature spiritually, we experience a greater disquiet as we ache for his presence to fill us and transfigure each facet of our distracted existence. Having tasted of God's goodness, we crave all the more. Not satisfied with a few drops, we desire to drink our fill from the promised streams of living water.

This thirst is as it should be. Entering a living relationship with other people does not satiate our desire to know them or love them. Rather, true friendship draws us into further fellowship. When we're continually learning new things, we appreciate others more fully. When we find that we are accepted and cherished for who we are, we long to share ourselves on a whole new plane. So it is in our walk with God.

The deeper spiritual life is available to all genuine believers. It is not an ideal reserved for a handful of elite Christians but a reality for all serious followers of Christ. Jesus summons us to a simplified and sanctified way of being. He calls us to substantive spiritual growth that transforms our human fallenness, heals our brokenness and restores us from the inside out. Ultimately Jesus welcomes us into intimate communion with himself and thereby into unfathomable fellowship with God the Father. We are invited to participate in the very love relationship that the Father and Son share from all eternity.

ONE THING

Such a life must of necessity be centered on one thing. Vibrant faith mandates a singular focus that provides clarity and motivation for all we do. As the psalmist exclaims, "One thing I ask of the LORD, this is what I seek. . . . Your face, LORD, I will seek" (Psalm 27:4, 8). The Lord's face, his personal friendship with us, is to be our singular obsession, the center of our existence. This is what we will seek. While we continue to live in the real world, fulfill our responsibilities and enjoy relationships, we need not become scattered and fragmented. Despite the distracted, multitasking culture that surrounds us, we can maintain our undivided focus on the Lord.

When Jesus visits the home of Martha and Mary in Bethany in Luke 10:38-42, Martha busies herself with meal arrangements to the point that she has no time for the Lord. She is "distracted by all the preparations" that need to be made and ultimately blames her sister—as well as Jesus—for ignoring her plight. Like many of us, Martha tries so earnestly to do the right things that she misses what is truly important. "Martha, Martha," replies Jesus, "you are worried and upset about many things, but only one thing is needed. Mary has chosen what is better, and it will not be taken away from her."

THIRSTY BELIEVERS

Longing for a deeper communion with Christ, many believers today are seeking spiritual direction, and many are discovering the wisdom offered by godly exemplars from the past twenty centuries of the church. This book welcomes us on an adventure with the Lord as it introduces us to the lives and devotional writings of some extraordinary women of God known as the Beguines. The entire lifestyle of these women revolved around the cultivation of an intimate relationship with Jesus.

One of the women we will meet in this book, Mechthild of Magdeburg, describes the spiritual longing that she feels in her whole being. Her words help to articulate the inner ache many of us experience:

> Lord, the desire I have for you when you draw me up,
> Lord, the wisdom I then receive in the flights of love,
> Lord, the union I then grasp in your will,
> Lord, the constancy I then preserve as your gift,
> Lord, the sweet remembrance when I think of you,
> Lord, the pampering love that I feel for you,
>
> is so rich in itself and is in your divine eyes so great . . . [that
> no one could] make clear to you even half of the intensity of

my longing and the pain of my suffering and my heart's pursuit and my soul's striving for the fragrance of your balsam, to hang inseparably in your embrace forever.[1]

The Beguines epitomize the pursuit of one thing: loving Jesus with their whole heart. From this singular focus emerge their creative initiative, vibrant friendship, study of Scripture and service to others. Their faith engages not only their hearts but also their heads and their hands.

Noteworthy women of faith, the Beguines provide a pattern for believers in our day seeking profound Christian spirituality. These medieval women model for us a radical relationship with Jesus that pervades every facet of life. Their narrative demonstrates uncommon faith and courageous action. While our circumstances may differ from those of these saintly ladies from the past, we can learn from their passion and their perseverance in discipleship.

THE BEGUINES CALL US TO COME

Our journey toward a deeper life in this book will be guided by this remarkable group of women. Their example calls us to cultivate spiritual friendships as well as to embrace growth that comes from trials and dry times in the desert. Above all, the Beguines welcome believers into an intimate friendship with Jesus.

Hadewijch is another of the early Beguines. In a letter to a young sister in Christ, Hadewijch invites her friend—and all of us who have the privilege to read her letters—to nurture an affectionate relationship with the Lord:

O beloved, why has not Love sufficiently overwhelmed you and engulfed you in her abyss? Alas! when Love is so sweet, why do you not fall deep into her? And why do you not touch God deeply enough in the abyss of his Nature, which is so unfathomable? Sweet love, give yourself for Love's sake fully to God in love.[2]

That invitation to spiritual intimacy echoes over the centuries to all thirsty hearts today. Let us not settle for bland faith or lose courage along the journey. Rather, like these devout women of bygone days, let our spiritual formation pulsate with passion for the Lord as we release control of our lives and seek him with all our heart, soul, mind and strength. Let us glean from their example and listen to their counsel as we drink from springs of living water and pursue a deeper life in Christ.

1

The Beguines

Believers Following Hard After God

O God, You are my God;
Early will I seek You;
My soul thirsts for You;
My flesh longs for You
In a dry and thirsty land
Where there is no water. . . .
My soul follows close behind You;
Your right hand upholds me.

Psalm 63:1, 8 (NKJV)

O Lord, if it could ever happen to me that I might gaze upon you as my heart
desires and hold you in my arms, then the divine pleasures of your love would
needs permeate my soul to the degree possible for people on earth. What I would
be willing to suffer thereafter has never been seen by human eyes. Indeed, a
thousand deaths were too little. Such, Lord, is my painful longing for you!

Mechthild of Magdeburg

Rising before daybreak, the young woman quickly dresses and hurries to meet the other members of her household for the morning Scripture reading. She cannot wait to hear the Bible read in her native language! Thirsty for more of the Lord each day, she loves to soak in God's Word and treasure it in her heart.

After the morning reading she returns to her room to work quietly by herself as she reflects on the passage. Throughout the day she meditates on the day's Scripture as she works at the linen press stationed to the side of her small quarters. Every time she places a piece of linen on the press she repeats a key verse from the morning's reading. As she dips each article of cloth into water, she immerses her thoughts anew in the living Word.

At noon she partakes of lunch by herself in order to maintain her focus on what God is teaching her. She sits quietly by the tall cupboard nestled in the far corner of her room. The top third of the cupboard holds the dishes she brought from her parents' home, the bottom third serves as her pantry, and the middle opens out into a small table. As she eats the unadorned meal of bread and cheese, she takes the morning Bible reading and turns it into her prayer for the day.

Throughout the afternoon she continues to reflect on God's Word. In the evening she once again gathers with the community members for the evening Scripture reading. After vespers she finds her closest friend, who has spent the day serving in the hospital nearby. They chat for a while and then turn their attention to things more serious: What has God been teaching them? How are their lives being transformed?

After praying with her spiritual sister, the young woman returns to her room for personal reflection. How thankful she is that she can be part of this Christian household. She moved into the community with these devout women to learn God's Word. What a privilege it is for her to hear Scripture read morning and evening and then to meditate on it all day long. She also came here to form spiritual friendships, and indeed she has been blessed, both with her close friend and the mentorship she receives from the spiritual director of the household. In short, she has come here to pursue God with all her heart, and that is what she is doing day after day.

Before retiring for the night, the young woman takes time to pray at the wooden kneeler alongside her bed. Her desire for Christ runs deep. Tomorrow will be a new opportunity to hear God's Word and to cultivate her intimate relationship with Jesus.

The place: Belgium. The year: 1200.

THE BEGUINES

During the two decades before the opening of the thirteenth century, middle class women across Belgium, the Netherlands, northern France and Germany began to establish Christian households where women could pursue a life of spiritual growth. Sisters, mothers, aunts and friends pooled their resources to buy large homes in emerging towns across Europe, and here they gathered to live with like-minded women of the faith. These devout laywomen were called Beguines.[1]

This was the height of the Middle Ages. Kings and queens reigned while knights jousted to prove their loyalty to their ladies. Europe's armies had launched two crusades, conquering Jerusalem and gaining territory in Palestine as they sought to protect Europe in the ongoing struggle between Christendom and Islam. Minstrels praised noblemen for their gallantry and sang of the unrequited love endured by women of the castle. Towns in the northern European lowlands and along the Rhine River flourished due to growing commerce and booming textile production. Although most of Europe was Christian, at least in name, many hungered for a more personal faith that they could live day to day.[2]

During this time a young woman named Mary of Oignies established one of the first Beguine communities in Belgium. Shortly after her marriage, Mary and her husband John consecrated their lives to work with lepers. Soon women began to gather around Mary and her ministry. Mary and these women of kindred spirit formed a loose community and were among the first wave of women to experience a spiritual renewal that would soon flood northern Europe in the age of chivalry.

Similar groups were forming in nearby towns, often following the same pattern: one woman of God engaging in outreach followed by others who desired to help her and learn from her. Although some of the women associated with the early Beguine communities were married, these groups primarily consisted of widows and single maids who had moved to the towns of northern Europe to find employment. Men were fewer in number because of the crusades, and many women needed to provide for themselves. Beguine houses offered a safe environment in which to live and work as well as an atmosphere conducive to spiritual growth. Not content with institutional religion, women dedicated their lives to Jesus.

The Beguine movement gained strong support from James of Vitry, a priest who was elevated to become bishop and then cardinal of the church. James knew firsthand the vibrant faith and deep devotion of these women, having received spiritual direction and encouragement from Mary while living in the town of Oignies. He helped to secure papal approval for the Beguines, as well as chronicling Mary's life and the early years of the movement. James described the early development of these households:

> Many holy maidens . . . scorned the temptations of the flesh, despised the riches of the world for the love of the heavenly bridegroom in poverty and humility, earning a sparse meal with their own hands. Although their families were wealthy, they preferred to endure hardship and poverty, leaving behind their family and their father's home rather than to abound in riches or to remain in danger amidst worldly pomp.[3]

These laywomen were first known simply as *mulieres religiosae* ("spiritual women") or *mulieres sanctae* ("holy women"). Later they were referred to as Beguines. Although no one knows for sure how the name emerged, a number of theories are in circulation, the most plausible being that the word was derived from the Old French *bèguer*, meaning "to stammer," since these women were known for ecstatic prayer as well as public preaching.[4] Whatever the source, it is clear that the term began as a pejorative one. Within a few decades, however, Beguines were respected for their chaste lifestyle and service to the poor. The derogatory overtones of the title faded away, and *Beguine* became the standard word for women living in Christian community without becoming members of an established religious order.

Unlike nuns, Beguines took no permanent vows. The communities provided unprecedented opportunity for spiritual formation, offering a middle ground between monastic seclusion and the active life in the world.[5] Beguines remained laywomen who were committed to celibacy and obedience to the household rules as long as they remained in the beguinage. They were free to leave the community if they chose, and some did in order to marry. This meant, however, that they had to relinquish the home they had helped to build. Therefore the vast majority of women who joined the Beguines remained in the community with its common way of life.

During the early thirteenth century, hundreds of Beguine communities were formed, especially in Belgium and Germany. Most accommodated about a dozen women, with one older sister serving as mistress and spiritual director for the household. As many as ten thousand of these devout women lived in German-speaking territories, with the city of Strasbourg boasting one thousand Beguines and Cologne two thousand (see map, p. 87).

WOMEN IN LOVE WITH JESUS

Unashamedly in love with Jesus, the Beguines pursued a singular devotion to him. One of their number, Mechthild of Magdeburg, expressed her passion for Jesus thus:

> I delight in loving him who loves me, and I long to love him

to the death, boundlessly, and without ceasing. Be happy, my
soul, for your Life has died for love of you. Love him so
fiercely that you could die for him. Thus you burn ever more
without ever being extinguished as a living flame in the vast
fire of high majesty.[6]

Athirst for Jesus, these women established households where they
could grow spiritually and pursue a deeper life in the Lord. That
pursuit included several facets.

First, many of the early Beguine communities came together
around the common task of ministering to the sick. They sought
to serve Jesus by serving the needy, providing medical care for the
sick and offering comfort to the terminally ill. In doing so they
organized some of the first hospitals in Europe. There were the
leprosaria led by Mary of Oignies as well as other facilities established just before the year 1200. In the city of Leuven, a group of
women who served the infirmary developed into a community of
some three hundred Beguines over the coming decades. Hand in
hand with service to the sick came care of the dying and preparation of bodies for burial. Hospice work became the Beguines' spe-
cialty. In time the term *Beguine* became virtually synonymous
with the tending of lepers, feeding of the hungry and caring for
the dying.

Second, very few individuals or families in the Middle Ages
owned a Bible. Copied by hand, volumes of Scripture were expen-
sive and rare, and those who wanted to learn God's Word needed
to join a spiritual community. So the Beguines combined their
resources, purchasing Bibles in addition to buildings. At the time,
the Scriptures were being translated into the vernacular languages
of Europe for the very first time. Although the church hierarchy
was wary of these popular translations since they were not always
accurate, it allowed them to be used for personal devotion and
public evangelism.[7] Many of the young women who joined Be-

guine communities were able to read and write in the common languages, and each day they would gather in a large room to hear Scripture read. Because these gatherings were the only times when they had access to a Bible, many women would virtually memorize each day's passage and reflect on it throughout the day.

Another reason women became Beguines was so they could enjoy fellowship with other fervent followers of Christ. Young women sought wise older sisters to mentor them in the faith and provide direction and encouragement along the way. It is of little wonder that so many hungry believers joined the Beguines as the movement blazed across northern Europe.

Finally, and above all, the Beguines created communities where they could cultivate an intimate relationship with Christ. Their households offered them sufficient space and solitude to pursue a recollected life. The Beguines were ardently in love with the Lord, and rather than using the term "personal relationship" as we might today, they employed the language of intimacy, viewing themselves as brides of Christ. Hadewijch of Brabant articulates their dedication:

> Oh, it is truly fitting, if anyone belongs exclusively to his Beloved, that his Beloved, in return, belong exclusively to him! As the Bride says in the Song of Songs: My Beloved to me, and I to him! (Song 2:16). Oh, to whom else should anyone belong exclusively but to his Beloved?[8]

SIMPLICITY

The Beguines sought to live lives of simplicity with regard to material possessions so they would have resources available to give to others. Well-to-do women gave away their possessions to help the less fortunate. Even the many poorer Beguines who eventually joined the movement donated to the needy as they were able. As one observer in their day noted, "In those houses many are so

poor that they have nothing but their bed and chest of clothes, but
they are burdensome to no one; by working with their hands . . .
they earn so much daily that they not only derive a modest liveli-
hood but they . . . give alms [to those in need]."[9]

Other women earned a living and served the community by
teaching children, especially poor girls who had no other possibility of receiving a basic education. The Beguines became well-
known as teachers. They established their own schools for girls
and taught them not only the basics of reading, writing and arith-
metic, but also Christian character. At one point the school in
Antwerp had fifty-seven girls living with the Beguines and receiving instruction.[10] These schools were so popular that the large
beguinage of Leuven eventually had to limit the number of schools
there to ten.[11]

EXPLOSION

The Beguine movement, which had begun as a few scattered gatherings of laywomen, soon mushroomed. In the 1230s and 1240s,
women joined the Beguines first by the hundreds and then by the
thousands. Catapulting the movement forward, Pope Gregory
IX—a good friend of James of Vitry—gave his written approval on
May 30, 1233, for women to continue forming these communities.
This papal support not only provided official recognition, it gave
the Beguines legal support. In some locales jealous clergy resisted
this newfangled Christian lifestyle and sought to close down Beguine households; in other areas town councils wanted to tax
their communities. Papal approval helped the Beguines hold their
ground against such opposition.

The second development that opened the door for the Beguines'
rapid growth was the donation of land and funding from members
of the nobility who appreciated the work these Christian women
were doing. Johanna, countess of Flanders, and her sister Margaret
contributed tremendous sums of money in the two decades after

1234 to establish and sustain Beguine communities in a dozen towns across Flanders.[12] Likewise, the dukes of Brabant supported the beguinage of La Vigne (The Vineyard) in Brussels and other communities across the duchy.[13] These endowments were substantial because most Beguine complexes held several hundred women. Other members of the landed gentry, as well as several bishops and abbots, made similar donations. The support of these key figures further buttressed the Beguines' legal position.

With these open doors, the Beguine movement exploded. So great was the spiritual thirst for community that within two decades, Belgium alone was home to well over ten thousand Beguines. In addition to more than a hundred smaller Beguine houses there, some sixty Beguine complexes held over a hundred women each. Three of these complexes were of enormous proportion. St. Elizabeth's beguinage in Ghent, founded by Countess Johanna, housed seven hundred women by the late 1200s. St. Christophe's in Liège numbered one thousand women, and the Great Beguinage in the city of Mechelen eventually held between fifteen hundred and nineteen hundred Beguines.[14]

EVANGELICAL AWAKENING

The Beguines were part of a massive evangelical awakening in the twelfth and thirteenth centuries that spawned a series of revivals across Europe and led to the establishment of a variety of new orders, not the least of which was that of St. Francis. In fact, Francis of Assisi was so intrigued by the saintly women of Belgium who lived together in Christian community that he attempted to visit the district where Mary of Oignies had lived. Unfortunately, he was unable to make the journey, but it is clear from his interest that he felt great affinity for their cause.

The evangelical awakening that gave birth to the Beguines, the Franciscans and other movements had begun a century earlier as clergy and laypeople alike began to experience a spiritual renewal

and commit themselves to a gospel lifestyle.[15] Although Europe
had been spiritually dry for hundreds of years, the first sparks of
revival ignited as a host of devout monks and hermits came out of
seclusion and began to proclaim the gospel in town and countryside alike.

These evangelical preachers painted a new portrait of Christ.
Rather than presenting him primarily as a vengeful king at the
Last Judgment, they offered a Jesus who reached out to humanity
and a Good Shepherd who drew the lost to himself. As they criss-
crossed Europe proclaiming the good news in various local languages, itinerant evangelists welcomed the crowds into a personal,
transformational encounter with the Lord. Many people heard the
gospel message for the first time. Although little is known of it
today, this spiritual renewal brought untold numbers into a vital
relationship with Christ.

Perhaps one of the most significant figures during this time
was the fiery preacher Bernard of Clairvaux. An influential early
leader of the Cistercian Order, Bernard toured France and beyond
calling people to personal conversion, exhorting them to leave
their worldly ways and material pursuits in order to surrender
their hearts to Christ. Using the biblical imagery of Christ as the
bridegroom and the church as his bride, the abbot of Clairvaux
invited his hearers into a love relationship with God, who is love
himself, and depicted a tender encounter with Jesus.

About the same time that Bernard was preaching, Robert of
Arbrissel was also traveling around France drawing large crowds
and summoning nominal Christians to a sanctified lifestyle and
genuine pursuit of the Lord. His followers became known as the
"Poor in Christ" and soon formed the Order of Fontevrault.

Two decades later, the priest Norbert of Xanten began to rove
about, calling clerics as well as laypeople to repentance. Because
keeping a concubine was common for clergy in that time, many
of Norbert's fellow priests resisted his message. However, he re-

ceived papal permission for his itinerant ministry and traversed Belgium, France and Germany, leading thousands to a vibrant walk with Christ. So many people began to follow him that he was forced to found a new monastic order, the Premonstratensians, or Order of Prémontré.

Women in particular responded to the invitations of Bernard, Robert, Norbert and the other itinerant preachers. Young and old, they joined communities where they could live side by side with other sincere believers and commit themselves to lives of prayer and spiritual devotion. Thousands sought to enter the Cistercian Order because of its moral integrity and the robust spirituality nourished by the bridal imagery of Bernard of Clairvaux.

Multitudes also poured into houses tied to Fontevrault and Prémontré. Fontevrault and the Premonstratensians were unique for their time in that they received women from all levels of society, not just those of noble birth. In fact, Fontevrault convents were known to have more than a few former prostitutes living alongside ladies of the nobility.[16] And as one observer of the Premonstratensian movement noted:

> The power of Christ [is] working in wondrous fashion—we daily see women, not only farmers' daughters or the poor, but even rich and noble widows and young girls, who after scorning the pleasures of the world hasten to these monasteries for the sake of conversion . . . so that we think that today there are more than ten thousand women in them.[17]

Soon all of these cloisters were filled to capacity and closed their doors to new members. Nevertheless, revival continued to spread. By the mid-twelfth century, another priest, Lambert le Bègue of Liège, in present-day Belgium, stepped forward as a revivalist preacher. He likewise summoned the clergy to renounce their immoral lifestyle, repent and turn to a true life of serving God. In addition, he translated portions of Scripture into Dutch—

Middle Flemish—so that common people could have God's Word in the language they understood. Some priests joined ranks with Lambert, along with a large following of laywomen.

Spiritual renewal was also catching fire elsewhere in Europe. In southern France members of the Waldensian movement spread the gospel from town to town and translated portions of the Bible into local dialects. Because the Waldensians' preaching threatened many local bishops, they were eventually excommunicated from the church and became what some consider the first Protestants. Some twenty years later, just after 1200, the two great orders of friars were founded: the Dominicans and the Franciscans. Like all of the renewal communities, they were often resisted by local clergy and bishops, who felt that the itinerant preachers were encroaching on their turf. Despite opposition, throngs of people came to faith in Christ through their ministry.

All of these evangelical movements, including the Beguines, were characterized by a clear conversion message and ministry to others. Their walk with Christ began with inner repentance and the renunciation of worldly ways, especially worldly wealth.[18] During this time trade was rapidly expanding in Europe, and the merchant middle class was amassing unprecedented wealth, often through unethical practices. Instead of caring for the needy, these merchants often squandered their newfound fortunes on their own pleasures. In protest, thousands of genuine believers renounced their inheritance and committed themselves to the *vita evangelica*—the evangelical lifestyle or gospel way of life. They sought to follow Jesus' instruction to the twelve when he commanded them to preach the gospel, taking "nothing for the journey—no staff, no bag, no bread, no money, no extra tunic" (Luke 9:3). In obedience, many sincere Christians abandoned their family's fortunes, donated their wealth to the poor and turned to follow Jesus.

Believers of the evangelical movements also dedicated themselves to public evangelism and practical service. Men, such as the Franciscan friars, traversed the highways and byways of Europe preaching the gospel two by two, just as the seventy-two were sent by Jesus in Luke 10:1-24. Although such travel would have been dangerous for women, the Beguines also engaged in active ministry, usually closer to home. Inviting other women to join their communities—and at times preaching publically—they called people to repentance and conversion from a worldly lifestyle. Such evangelism was always coupled with practical service to the poor and infirm, especially the colonies of lepers found near many of the towns in Europe.

BEGUINES OVER THE CENTURIES

The Beguines flourished for many decades and then began to wane. By the end of the thirteenth century they had come under suspicion. Some of their number, especially those who refused to be incorporated into the larger Beguine communities, had apparently been propagating some of the false teachings attributed to the Brethren of the Free Spirit. These teachings emphasized personal direction from the Holy Spirit over the guidance of Scripture, rejected church authority and the sacraments, and claimed that followers were free from the moral restrictions enumerated in the New Testament.[19] Because of these occasional ties with heresy, the Beguines were condemned at the Council of Vienne in 1311–1312. The council's statement exempted Beguines who were living in community and not connected with the Free Spirit, but the Vienne condemnation still undermined the movement, especially in Germany. It declined substantially during the fourteenth century.

During the spread of Protestantism in the sixteenth and seventeenth centuries, Beguine communities experienced a significant renaissance in Catholic territories. The movement also experienced a small resurgence in the nineteenth century, when a new, large beguinage was built outside the city of Ghent. But the secularization of the twentieth century led to the closing of most beguinages, and today only a handful of Beguines are left in Belgium. Nevertheless, a number of the large Beguine complexes still stand in cities across that country. Some have been converted into quiet neighborhoods of private townhomes. Others are run by public welfare services and provide housing to the underprivileged. In 1998 UNESCO adopted thirteen Beguine complexes as world heritage sites and preserved them as historical landmarks for all to see.

Although after eight centuries the Beguines have virtually disappeared as a movement, their invitation to a deeper spiritual life lives on. By their example and through their writing, these radical believers welcome us into an intimate oneness with God—begun in this life and consummated at the great wedding feast in heaven.

REMARKABLE MODELS OF FAITH

In this volume we will meet four key women related to the Beguine movement. Mary of Oignies served as ministry leader and spiritual model for one of the earliest communities established in Belgium. She offers an outstanding example of initiative and desire.

The other three women leave written legacies that provide insights regarding the path of spiritual growth. Penned as guidebooks to encourage sisters in the Beguine communities, these writings offer us direction for our journey and challenge us to go further in our spiritual formation. All of these writings are available today in English translation, as noted in the Suggestions for Further Reading at the end of this book. Beatrice of Nazareth, who was taught by the Beguines and eventually became a Cistercian nun, leads us on an exploration of the various seasons of the soul as she describes seven stages of a love relationship with God.

Mechthild of Magdeburg depicts our inner longings for the Lord and guides us in our quest to balance our solitary times of devotion with active service to others. She calls us to embrace suffering in this life as part of our pilgrimage.

Hadewijch of Brabant details the experience of spiritual sweetness as we fall in love with Jesus. She bids us encounter this sweetness with Jesus and assures us that the frustrations we face on our pilgrimage will ultimately lead us into the Promised Land, the oneness with the Lord for which our hearts long:

> But, O free, noble, and highborn souls,
> Not only called but chosen,
> Spare no trouble or pain in your approach
> To live in the ardor of lofty fidelity!
> Let your whole life be holy affliction,
> Until you are master of your Beloved.
>
> O hearts, let not your many griefs
> Distress you! You shall soon blossom;
> You shall row through all storms,
> Until you come to that luxuriant land
> Where Beloved and loved one shall wholly flow
> through each other.[20]

Through their writings the Beguines offer spiritual guidance to believers today, helping us negotiate the twists and turns of our own spiritual pilgrimage. They caution us against placing too much emphasis on extraordinary experiences and feelings that fade over time. They also describe seasons of suffering and show us how God is at work in our lives through the most difficult times. As spiritual directors, these women of intense faith offer us courage during desert times and hope of renewed spiritual intimacy as we walk with the Lord.

Personal Response
Drinking from Springs of Living Water

Reflection and Journaling

Where do you see spiritual dryness, questionable leadership or need of awakening in the church today?

Although your setting may be very different than the Beguines', in what ways can you promote genuine faith in your life situation?

On a personal level, how can you seek spiritual renewal for your own life?

Scripture

Read Psalm 63 out loud. The King James Version beautifully translates verse 8: "My soul followeth hard after thee." How are you following hard after God in your life?

Read afresh the account of Mary and Martha in Luke 10:38-42. What are the "many things" in your life that you, like Martha, tend to worry about? How are they distracting you from focusing on Jesus? Describe how you also desire the Lord and seek him as the "one thing" above all else in life. How can you cultivate a life like Mary's?

Creativity and Action

Take an hour's stroll with the Lord this week and talk with God about your current relationship with him. Where is that friendship life-giving? Where have the initial flames grown dim? What invitation is he extending to you at this point in your life?

On a sheet of paper, express what you see when you consider a deeper life in Christ. Perhaps you will sketch a picture, or maybe you will write down some words. Indeed, you might use a combination of both. What does it mean to daily abide in Jesus? How does your heart long for a more profound experience of him?

Community

Who are the people you are growing with spiritually? If you do not currently have someone with whom you share your inner life, who might you ask? How can you gather with some like-minded friends in your pursuit of God?

2

Radical Faith

Mary of Oignies Takes Initiative

From the days of John the Baptist until now, the kingdom of heaven has been forcefully advancing, and forceful men [and women] lay hold of it.

MATTHEW 11:12

The law of Love is to be obedient. . . . [The noble soul] is subject to no one save Love alone, who holds him fettered in love. No matter what anyone else would have said, he speaks according to Love's will. And he does service and performs the works of Love according to her will night and day in all liberty, without delay or fear and without counting the cost.

HADEWIJCH OF BRABANT

THE SUN SHONE ON THE BELGIAN countryside as Mary recited her vows to the young man named John. Mary came from a well-to-do family in the town of Nivelles, and, as most marriages in her day, hers had been arranged by her parents. The year was 1190, and Mary was fourteen years old.

Because John's family was also wealthy, the couple lived comfortably, and the first several months of their life together were unremarkable. All of this changed dramatically, however, because of Mary's passionate commitment to Christ. Unwilling to settle for complacent Christianity and a life of leisure, Mary chose to radically follow Jesus.

Mary took initiative in many ways. She stepped away from a lifestyle of wealth and comfort, realizing that it could easily distract her from a passionate pursuit of Christ. She approached John and encouraged him to join her in the venture and dedicate their lives together to the Lord's service. Taking an extraordinary step of faith, they gave all of their possessions to the poor. They laid aside their position of privilege to pursue a life of prayer and ministry to others. Rather than moving apart from each other to enter separate convents, as was the custom for godly couples in the Middle Ages, Mary and John remained together and devoted themselves to seeking the Lord and serving the infirm as a couple.

EXHAUSTING WORK AND POWERFUL PRAYER

Mary also took initiative as she ministered among the neediest of the needy. In the cluster of towns south of Brussels where Mary lived, she did not need to look far to find the leper colony of Williambroux. This was the field where she and John rolled up their sleeves and put their hand to the plow. Like Mother Teresa and the Sisters of Charity in our own time, Mary ministered to both the lepers' physical and spiritual needs. James of Vitry tells us, "From the abundant piety of her heart she therefore busied herself as far as she was able in the external works of mercy . . . [occupying] herself above all in assisting the sick and being present at death beds for contrition or at burials."[1]

The stench of decaying flesh would have filled John and Mary's nostrils day after day as they bandaged the lepers' open sores. Far from the affluence they had known in their youth, the couple centered their life about the basic care of the sick and dying. Flirting with the possibility of contracting disease themselves, Mary and John remained content to serve Christ by salving the wounds of the neediest of the needy.

Because John and Mary gave away their inheritance to provide for the poor and sick, they assumed the task of supporting themselves while they served in their mission, subsisting on the meager wages they could earn working with their hands. After a day attending to lepers, Mary often stayed up half the night to spin and sew, making enough income to provide the basic necessities of food and clothing for herself, her husband and those they ministered to.

During the long hours at night as Mary worked to support herself and the ministry, she interceded for those in need. She prayed for people with a wide spectrum of needs. Time and again she saw the Lord miraculously answer her petition and heal their lives.

One young woman Mary prayed for was a Cistercian nun with depression. This woman's despair was so great that she believed she had lost her faith in God and attempted suicide numerous times. Mary's heart was filled with compassion when she met the young nun, so she began praying for her and undertook a forty-day fast on her behalf. By the end of this time the woman was free of the demonic harassment that had plagued her for so long. Mary interceded for many who struggled with depression or were oppressed by evil spirits. Her biographer wrote, "When the enemy had drawn his bow 'to shoot in the dark the upright of heart' [Psalm 11:2], she was not content with tears or prayers but she would begin to fast, for she knew that this kind of demon was not easily driven out except by fasting and prayer (cf. Mk. 9:28)."[2]

At times Mary saw miraculous healings when she laid her hands on those she prayed for. Her biography records one incidence of a boy in Oignies who was bleeding from the ear. No medical treatment had helped, so he was brought to Mary. When Mary prayed for him he was "perfectly restored to health by the medicine of her prayers and by the laying on of hands."[3]

SPIRITUAL DIRECTION

John and Mary were not alone in their work among the lepers. Word of Mary's ministry and spiritual passion traveled quickly, and soon other women joined them at Williambroux. Creating an informal community, these women risked their lives to feed and dress the sick and dying in the leper colony. At the same time they were mentored by Mary. Daily they observed her example of prayer and listened to her instruction on the spiritual life. Mary proved to be a tremendous model as well as a spiritual mother to the women who gathered around her, and she offered wisdom and insight from the Lord for their lives. Thus began one of the first Beguine communities in Belgium.

The number of people asking for Mary's attention, however, eventually overwhelmed her. Over time, the days spent nursing the sick and the late nights spinning and praying took their toll. After some fifteen years among the lepers, Mary retreated from public ministry.[4] Physically weary and spiritually longing for solitude, she moved into a secluded room near the church in the town of Oignies. During these last years of her life, Mary pursued prayer with abandon. She still occasionally visited the sick and comforted the dying, but she spent much more time in Scripture and enjoying intimacy with her Savior. Often she devoted herself to intercessory prayer, battling for the lives and souls of friends and strangers alike.

In these times of prayer Mary would sometimes receive discernment or warnings from the Lord for people around her. "How often she forewarned her intimate friends of dangers!" writes James of Vitry. "How often she detected the hidden traps of the evil spirits to help her friends! How often she strengthened the faint-hearted and those wavering in faith by wondrous divine revelations! How often she warned others not to perform some thing which they were privately planning to do! How often she lightened the burdens [of] those who were falling into sin and almost in despair by divine consolations!"[5]

While less active than her years among the lepers, Mary's season of semiseclusion proved to be her most fruitful in terms of spiritual influence on the church in Belgium and eventually all of Europe. Despite her solitude, the fruit of her ministry increased. She preached, calling nominal Christians to commit their lives to Christ. She also provided spiritual direction for key men and women around her. Often people who met Mary were touched by God's presence. Some were convicted of their worldly ways and came to repentance. Others were comforted in their distress and sorrow. Giles, the pastor of the Beguines in Nivelles (and Mary's brother-in-law) sought her for spiritual counsel. Various clergy followed suit and came to Mary for guidance because they recognized her godly lifestyle, her obvious wisdom and her deep relationship with Jesus.

News of Mary's sanctified life and spiritual insight spread far and wide. In Paris a theology student named James of Vitry heard about Mary and moved to Oignies to live with other priests and be close to her. Through Mary the Lord provided James with a model of a holy life, as well as encouragement in ministry. Due in large part to her inspiration, he soon emerged as a powerful preacher who called thousands to Christ. God revealed to Mary that James would be asked to become a bishop, and she encouraged him to take the position. In time James rose to the position of cardinal, counseling the pope who gave official recognition to the Beguines and their communities.

In fact, it was through James of Vitry that Mary's greatest legacy was realized. James wrote Mary's first spiritual biography, *The Life of Mary of Oignies*, which presented her life as an example to all who were spiritually thirsty. In the following years Mary's story influenced hundreds of women, stirring them to seek Christ and join Beguine houses. Much of what we know about the women's revival in these years comes from James's biography of Mary as

well as another work, *History of the West*, which describes the spiritual fire racing across Europe.

On June 23, 1213, Mary died at the age of thirty-six. Her lasting
effect was felt by all who knew her personally and those far and
wide who heard about her exemplary commitment to Christ. Mary
serves as a role model to this day.

BEGUINE INITIATIVE

As Mary's life shows us, Beguine spirituality entails initiative. One
of the most notable characteristics of Mary and the other Beguines
is that they took action. They stepped out of the tradition of their
day to form a new kind of Christian community and join with
like-minded laywomen. Unwilling to settle for the status quo of
the dry Christianity surrounding them, the Beguines pursued a
living relationship. They understood that they needed to cultivate
their spiritual life. They formed communities where they could
learn the Bible and read what few devotional materials were available in their local language.

While Beguine devotion was personal, it also reached out to
others. Genuine faith cannot remain a private affair. "What good
is it, my brothers, if a man claims to have faith but has no deeds?"
asks our Lord's brother. "Suppose a brother or sister is without
clothes and daily food. If one of you says to him, 'Go, I wish you
well; keep warm and well fed,' but does nothing about his physical
needs, what good is it?" (James 2:14-16).

The heavenly-mindedness of the Beguines did not detract from
their earthly-goodness. Jesus tells us that the way we have responded to the sick, the hungry, the thirsty, the naked—indeed, the
least of those around us—is how we have treated him. In a parable
he tells us that the returning King will say to those on his right:

Come, you who are blessed by my Father; take your inheritance, the kingdom prepared for you since the creation of the

world. For I was hungry and you gave me something to eat
. . . I needed clothes and you clothed me, I was sick and you
looked after me . . . whatever you did for one of the least of
these brothers of mine, you did for me. (Matthew 25:34-40)

It is one thing to see the hungry and naked; it is another to do
something about it. That takes initiative. The women of the twelfth
and thirteenth centuries were innovators. They displayed radical
love for Jesus, and they reached out to the poor and infirm in
radical ways. They conquered fear of contracting leprosy, and they
overcame the inertia of cultural expectations. Establishing hospitals, founding communities and offering education to young girls,
the Beguines broke all the stereotypes for women of the day.

Other Beguines, like Mechthild of Magdeburg and Hadewijch
of Brabant, took initiative in a different way: by writing devotional
books. This took tremendous courage for two reasons. First,
women were not recognized by medieval society as writers, particularly in the realm of spiritual matters. Second, the women
wrote in the common languages in a day when Latin was the language of the church. Instead of remaining quiet, these women
spearheaded a movement of writing in the vernacular. They took
the genre of love poetry in their day and transformed it into beautiful verse that invited many others into an intimate relationship
with Christ. They produced the first devotional works and first
spiritual formation manuals written by common believers for
common Christians in the common language.

JESUS' INVITATION WHEN WE ARE STUCK
Developing a vibrant walk with Jesus has always required initiative.
Initiative is essential in any relationship. God has already taken the
initial steps toward us. Out of love he sent his only Son to die for us
in order to reconcile us to himself (see especially 2 Corinthians 5:18-
21 and John 3:16). He has roused our hearts to hunger and thirst after

him, and he is wooing us to himself. Without such stirring of the
Holy Spirit in our hearts, we would never be drawn to seek him.

In response we must also take initiative. We cannot remain passive. A relationship in which one side remains inert is anything but
a full friendship. Both parties must engage their wills as well as
their hearts. Many of us face a problem, however. At times we find
ourselves stuck. Our legs seem to have sunk into primordial tar pits
and we cannot move forward. We become stagnant in our relationships. Perhaps we have no life-giving friendships around us and we
feel isolated and alone, or we are in a bad relationship that we know
we must get out of. We might feel trapped in our career. After years
of not moving forward, we have begun to lose hope for something
better for our future. Or we may be caught in our commitment to
some form of service or ministry that is going nowhere. This inertia
affects our walk with the Lord. Either we fail to take time to be with
God, or our devotion is flat and stale.

Often we find ourselves stuck in more than one area, when
"stuckness" describes our life in general. Work, relationships, ministry and church have all gone dry. We feel trapped on the merry-
go-round of life and we are clueless about how to get off. It is when
we are stuck that we most need to take some kind of initiative.
However, especially if we have been immobile for some time, taking initiative is the one thing that we are not sure how to do.

In the Gospels, many people set examples of initiative for us.
One is the woman in Mark 5 who has been hemorrhaging for
twelve years. This unnamed woman has spent all her money on
doctors to no avail, but now she has a new idea. She will find Jesus
in the crowd and touch the edge of his robe. Although she knows
she is ceremonially unclean and that the mob around Jesus could
stone her, she takes the initiative to find the Savior. Refusing to
remain in her present condition, she pushes past person after person in the crowd and stretches out her hand to tap the hem of
Jesus' robe. The instant she does, she is healed.

What do you want from the Lord? Jesus is asking you today: What is it that you desire? How badly do you long for it? If you desire a deeper walk with him, in what way can you seek a more intimate relationship? Be encouraged: If you long for a more meaningful friendship with the Lord, then he is already at work in your life. He has taken the first step to stir up a yearning in your heart and given you a glimpse of what that deeper relationship with him might look like. Now is the time for you to step forward.

Perhaps you desire to reach out to others. Often we envision social action and medical missions in heroic proportion—risking our lives in the slums of Calcutta or among inner city gangs. While places like these represent genuine need and some people are called to full-time service there, we cannot all relocate to such a mission field. However, we can all reach out to the needy around us. Mary did not travel far to find her ministry—it was simply the leper colony down the road. Such mission fields are often the least glamorous and the very ones we want to ignore. Yet those are the places where we must begin. Should God choose to move us to a more exotic locale, great. Should he keep us close to home, let us engage wholeheartedly in the world at hand.

When we are stuck, we must take initiative. We must be ready to take the step in front of us. Like Peter about to walk on water, we need to focus on that first step of getting out of the boat and not concern ourselves with what is next. Seldom does the Lord show us more than one step in front of us. Although we often want to see the whole itinerary, God gives us one piece of it at a time. By doing so, he keeps us from running off on our own, assuming that we can take care of ourselves.

FACING OPPOSITION

When we step out in obedience to God, we usually assume that the struggle is finished. More often than not, however, the battle intensifies. We must be prepared for opposition. Far from receiving encouragement from their families, Mary and John suffered ridicule from those closest to them when they chose a life of mission instead of comfort. "Worldly people, as well as their own relatives," recorded James of Vitry, "looked at them and gnashed their teeth against the persons whom they had honoured before when they were wealthy. The persons made poor for Christ's sake were now condemned and mocked."[6]

In similar fashion, many Beguines received a mixed welcome from their surrounding communities. While some townspeople and clergy appreciated their dedication to the Lord and service among the needy, others misunderstood them. Not everyone appreciated their rejection of wealth. Relatives recoiled at their desire to live celibate lives, and various clergy accused them of heresy, assuming that they were not competent to study the Bible.

Scripture is replete with examples of those who hit resistance as they obeyed God. When Moses confronted Pharaoh, the Egyptian king commanded the slaves to gather their own straw to make bricks, causing the Israelites to reject Moses' leadership. When blind Bartimaeus cried out for Jesus to have mercy on him, the crowd tried to silence him. When Jairus and his wife welcomed Jesus into their home to raise their daughter from the dead, the crowd mocked the idea of their daughter's recovery.

When we take initiative toward God, things often become worse before they become better. We need to be prepared for opposition and not give up. In all these examples from Scripture, men and women of faith persisted and did not crumble under opposition. Moses confronted Pharaoh with plagues until the Israelites were released. Bartimaeus shouted all the louder, and the Lord healed him. Jairus and his wife went with Jesus into their daughter's bedroom and saw her rise from the dead.

KEEPING OUR FOCUS ON GOD

When we do take initiative, we must be careful to focus on God.

Mary of Oignies placed no emphasis on herself. While she clearly demonstrated gifts of wisdom, healing, helps and even prophecy, she drew no attention to herself. She simply wanted to serve Jesus and to encourage the downcast, comfort the sick and draw all into a deeper walk with God. James of Vitry tells us that "she always strove to hide herself." In fact, she would rather have allowed others be used by the Lord instead of her. James continues, "How many times did she reply to God, almost as if she were grumbling, 'Why are you bothering me Lord? Send whom you must send. I am not worthy to go to declare your counsels to another.' Nevertheless she could not resist the stirring of the Holy Spirit because through it she could be of service for the help of others."[7]

Focus on God and compassion for others allowed Mary's ministry to take different shapes throughout her life. Early in her marriage, Mary ministered to the nearby lepers. In her later years, she served the Lord in solitude, interceding for people and offering spiritual direction to leaders around her. In each stage of her life, Mary pursued the Lord, and he channeled her ministry in a variety of ways.

Service to God may take a variety of forms during different seasons of our lives. While the Lord may use us in a given ministry for years, we will not necessarily maintain the same mission our whole life. Often different needs present themselves, and we recognize God's invitation to join him in meeting those needs. Or we simply find that we are in a new stage of life with a different focus of personal growth and compassionate outreach. We must find the right expression for our godly passions in each period. Some years may be dedicated more to prayer and intercession, while others may center about ministry to those in need. Another season is devoted to solitude and waiting on God, and still another focuses on mentoring other believers.

Mary and the early Beguines provide a model—and also a challenge—to contemporary Christians. Many of us want ministry, but we want it on our own terms. We follow the advice of a spiritual gift or temperament inventory, because we are told to pursue what comes naturally to us. However, neither Mother Teresa of the twentieth century nor Mary of Oignies in the twelfth chose what came easily to them. Instead they took time to listen to the Lord's leading in their lives. Then they joined God by ministering in the most humble of circumstances. They assumed the attitude of John the Baptist: "He must increase, but I must decrease" (John 3:30 NASB). Far from trying to self-actualize through ministry, they simply forgot themselves. In the midst of that self-forgetfulness, God chose to raise them up as models for the whole world to see.

Personal Response
Drinking from Springs of Living Water

Reflection and Journaling

In what ways do Mary and John inspire you or challenge you? Which aspects of their life would you like to emulate?

In what ways do you currently feel stuck in life? How has that inertia caused spiritual dryness in your life?

Are there ways that you have been trying to take initiative? What opposition have you come up against?

Scripture

Read Matthew 15:21-28. How can you be like Canaanite woman who took initiative to find Jesus and refused to take no for an answer?

Read Isaiah 58. God is not impressed by the Israelites' fasting and prayer for help because of their lack of concern for the oppressed in the land. In this chapter of Isaiah, who are the oppressed God is concerned about? How does this apply to us today?

Creativity and Action

Take initiative in one area of your life today. This could be establishing time with the Lord, connecting with a friend, tackling a responsibility you have been avoiding or reaching out to someone in need. Take one concrete step forward, no matter how small it may seem.

If you are not currently engaged in outreach of some kind, what group in your community or ministry in your church can you give a hand to? Has God placed certain people on your heart? They could be individuals in your town, orphaned children, inner city youth, girls caught in sex trade or innumerable others in need. What creative initiatives can you take to learn about them and to give the first gestures of assistance?

Community

Call a friend and tell her or him what steps of initiative you are beginning this week. Ask your friend to pray for you. Also ask him or her to check up on you next week so you do not back out of your commitment.

3

Desiring God's Presence

The Beguines Cultivate Prayer and Soak in Scripture

Above all else, guard your heart,
   for it is the wellspring of life.

PROVERBS 4:23

Jesus, dearest Lover of mine, let me approach you . . . with deep love for you in
my heart, and never let me grow cold, so that I constantly feel your intense love
in my heart and in my soul and in my five senses and in all my members. Then I
can never grow cold.

MECHTHILD OF MAGDEBURG

To touch God's presence—this was the passion of the Beguines.
Longing not only to know about the Lord in the abstract, Mary of
Oignies and the myriad of devout women who came after her desired to experience God's actual companionship. When we look at
the lives of these twelfth- and thirteenth-century women and read
their writings, we are struck by their passion for God's felt imma-
nence. As Mechthild of Magdeburg expresses in the quotation
above, they wanted to feel God's intense love in their heart, soul
and whole being.

The Beguines were unafraid to allow their hearts to desire. In fact, such openness to inner longing characterizes the movement as a whole. This yearning is evident in their writings. As Hadewijch exhorts, "You must leave all for all so exclusively, and burn so ardently in your soul, and in your being, and in all your works, that nothing else exists for you anymore but God alone—no pleasure and no pain, nothing easy and nothing difficult."[1]

DESIGNED TO DESIRE

Desire is the wellspring of our life. It provides the vigor that gives purpose to our lives and empowers us to overcome fatigue and frustration throughout the day. What we desire—what we treasure—directs our hearts. Jesus says, "For where your treasure is, there your heart will be also" (Matthew 6:21). To understand anyone, including ourselves, we must discover what that person desires. If we look carefully, we will discover that a person's actions, thoughts and attitudes spring from a deep inner longing.

Desire is what draws us out of ourselves and stirs us to reach out to other people and to God. Without it we would remain trapped within ourselves. As persons molded in the likeness of the three-personed God, we are created to long for "the other"—both human and divine. We are designed to desire God and to pursue him, to love the Lord with our whole heart, soul and body, and to enjoy intimate fellowship with him forever.

Our love for God is always in response to God's eternal initiative toward us. God loved the world so much that he reached out to us by giving us his Son. In John 15:16 Jesus asserts, "You did not choose me, but I chose you." Mechthild of Magdeburg recognized that her desire for the Lord was a response to his original desire for and initiative toward her:

Dear Lord, I cannot control my longing; I would so dearly like to be with you.

Our Lord said: "I longed for you before the beginning of the world. I long for you and you long for me. Where two burning desires meet, there love is perfect."[2]

Deep desire for God is not simply that which ushers us into a saving relationship with the Lord; it is the spiritual vitality that fills our lives year after year. Just as the romance between a man and woman should grow and not diminish when they engage and marry, so our lifelong connection with God is to be characterized by an unquenchable, ever-expanding love for him.

Our inner yearning is the fountainhead of a deeper spiritual life. It is our source of energy and the fire that empowers our pursuit of God. Without it we will never experience the intimacy with Jesus that we long for. While many of us as Christians claim to have invited the Lord into our lives, the question is, what do we long for today? Do we truly desire God?

GOD'S MANIFEST PRESENCE

The Beguines were women to whom God's presence was much more than a theological proposition. It was the fundamental reality of their lives and the focal point around which they organized all their activity. The Beguines recognized each divine encounter as a fresh "greeting" from the Lord, a chance for his divine presence to pour afresh into their soul. "This is a greeting that has many streams," says Mechthild. "It pours forth from the flowing God into the poor, parched soul unceasingly with new knowledge, in new contemplation, and in the special enjoyment of the new presence."[3]

But these thirsty women were not content to simply long for God's touch. They actively attended the Lord's presence. While they did not try to conjure up God's presence or control the Almighty, they recognized that they had a role to play. They needed to strip away distractions in their lives and make themselves present to the Lord. Especially through prayer and Scripture, they cultivated an intimate relationship with the divine.

A LIFE OF PRAYER

From her teenage years, Mary of Oignies spent the wee hours of the morning in prayer while she worked with her hands to support herself and the ministry. She loved these long hours of the night when she could soak in the Lord's presence. Besides interceding for others during her time of solitude, Mary often savored sweet communion with her Savior. Frequently as she prayed she was caught up in the Lord's presence. At times she dissolved in tears of sheer gratitude for Jesus' sacrifice on the cross. On other occasions she broke out into joyous celebration, spontaneously proclaiming songs of praise. This prayer life is what energized her manual labor and ministry to others.

Often Mary took time to meditate on the cross and Jesus' sacrifice for our sins. In fact, she was so moved by Christ's passion that she could not look at a cross in church without breaking into irrepressible tears. Above all she continually cultivated a personal communion with Jesus and love for him. As James of Vitry wrote, "Christ was for her a meditation in the heart, a word in the mouth, an example in her works."[4]

Like Mary, the Beguines as a whole were devoted to God in prayer. Rather than simply use the term "prayer," however, they referred to solitude with the Lord with a wide range of words to describe their relational intimacy: "enjoying God's presence," "savoring spiritual sweetness," "hearing God's greeting" and "receiving his kiss." Along with most of the devout believers of the Middle Ages, the Beguines depicted their encounter with God's presence in terms of bridal intimacy. Here is how Hadewijch articulates her desire for the One who died on the cross to forgive her sins:

Beloved, if I love a beloved,
Be you, Love, my Beloved;

You gave yourself as Love for your loved one's sake,
And thus you, Love, uplifted me, your loved one, with you!
O Love, were I but love,
And could I but love you, Love, with love!
O Love, for love's sake, grant that I,
Having become love, may know Love wholly as Love![5]

Hadewijch then instructs her readers, "Remain undivided and withhold yourself from all meddling with good or bad, high or low; let everything be, and keep yourself free to devote yourself to your Beloved and to content him whom you love in Love."[6]

The Beguines seldom if ever referred to prayer as a spiritual discipline. Spending time with God was not an obligation but a privilege. It was not an ascetic exercise to produce spiritual growth but rather the heartbeat of their relationship with the One they loved. The spiritual journey for them was one of deep desire rather than religious duty.

SAVORING SCRIPTURE

The Beguines also nurtured God's presence by soaking in his Word. Joining a Beguine house afforded women the opportunity to hear the Bible on a daily basis and offered them space where they could maintain their spiritual focus on Scripture throughout the day. Most Beguines enjoyed a peaceful environment in which to work and meditate, and they had like-minded sisters with whom they could share their insights from God's Word. One observer describes their life as follows:

> Rising early they meet at church. . . . When they have heard the mass and each has said her prayers, they return to their own houses and work in silence all day so that they never cease from prayer; or they repeat . . . Psalms which they know. Late in the evening after vespers, when they have leisure for prayer and meditation, they go again to church and then retire.[7]

For the Beguines, the deeper life was cultivated through Scripture. Like other believers in the Middle Ages, the Beguines gathered corporately each day in order to hear God's Word read. Then they practiced a fourfold rhythm of reading and reflecting on Scripture common to Christian communities in the Middle Ages referred to as *lectio divina*—"sacred reading" or "devotional reading."

The first rhythm was *lectio*—Latin for "reading"—in which they read or listened to God's Word. Usually a short passage was read aloud to the community several times through. The women would memorize it as best they could so that they could reflect on it throughout the day. In a culture, unlike ours, where books were not available, people developed their capacity to memorize far more than we do today. Thus it was not uncommon for them to learn chapters of Scripture by heart so that they could treasure it as they worked with their hands.

Meditatio was the second rhythm, a time when the women reflected and meditated on the day's Scripture. The Beguines continually repeated the verses to themselves, along with psalms and other biblical passages they knew. Picturing the events of a narrative, they would bring a passage to life in their mind's eye. While contemporary Christians often wait for a film like *The Passion of the Christ* to animate the events of Scripture in Technicolor, medieval believers employed their own imaginations to do the same.

Meditatio led naturally into *oratio*—"prayer." Members of medieval communities learned to take Scripture and turn it into petition. They would pray the passage over their lives, asking God to work his truth into their minds and hearts.

Finally, *lectio divina*—this longstanding pattern of Scripture immersion combined with prayer—flowed into *contemplatio*, or "contemplation." Simply stated, contemplation was the act of experiencing silent awe in God's presence. It was a solitary focus on the Lord himself. Rather than reflecting on the content of the passage, as in meditation, the Beguines simply focused on God's love and relished his loving presence.

SORTING THROUGH OUR DESIRES

How can we apply the Beguines' model of desiring God in our lives today? We must begin by examining our desires. What we desire is perhaps the most important component of our personal formation. Jesuit leader Pedro Arrupe phrases it beautifully:

> Nothing is more practical than finding God, than falling in love in a quite absolute, final way. What you are in love with, what seizes your imagination, will affect everything.
>
> It will decide what will get you out of bed in the morning, what you will do with your evening, how you spend your weekends, what you read, whom you know, what breaks your heart, and what amazes you with joy and gratitude. Fall in love, stay in love, and it will decide everything.[8]

Although God created us to desire, not all of our desires are godly. If we are honest, we will realize that our hearts harbor both devout and distorted wishes. In fact, some of what we long for is quite twisted. Scripture acknowledges this. Our faculty of desire became deformed in the fall. As a result we long for the wrong things. Every one of us ultimately pursues erroneous paths, as Romans 3:23 summarizes: "All have sinned and fall short of the glory of God."

With disordered hearts we are prone to crave created things instead of satisfying ourselves with the Creator. We chase after money and success; we pursue power and prestige. We cling to people and hope to find our security in them. We seek the comfortable life and search for entertainment and other stimuli of many kinds. We obsess over our body image and exercise compulsively in a futile attempt to remain young. Like Narcissus, we fixate on our own self-image until we drown in it. If we are truthful with ourselves, we quickly become aware that something within us is very broken. Unchecked, our fallen nature will cave in on itself.

Our desires also become distracted. In our hyper-paced culture, we are sidetracked by many demands, opportunities and constantly changing technologies. Some of the things we run after are not sinful per se, but because we place them before the Lord, they corrupt our affections. The television screen offers constant stimulation, challenging us to concentrate on any image for more than a few seconds. On our computer monitors half a dozen windows await our click while pop-ups flash more images attempting to captivate our attention. Multitasking characterizes our work and our leisure time as we engage in more and more activities, yet experience less and less peace. Our focus is dissipated and our lives are fragmented.

As believers we are not immune to these influences. Often our motives are mixed. We aspire to be people of prayer, and we want to taste everything the world has to offer. We want to serve others, and we want to receive recognition for it. We want to be humble, and we hope others notice our deep humility. In order to grow in Christ, we need to allow him to purify our hearts and purge away all that is scattered and ignoble. As we lay our inclinations before the Lord, we must be fully honest with him and with ourselves.

Such a warped condition is not how we were originally made. Although our affections are misdirected, we can experience the restoration of a healthy desire for God in our lives. Through Christ's atonement, our attention can be turned around and our inner orientation redeemed. The goal of the Christian life is not to destroy desire but to allow the Holy Spirit to purify our inner desires and direct them back toward God.

DARE TO DESIRE

When we compare the state of much of the contemporary church with the thousands of women swept up in the medieval revival, we become aware of our distraction and lukewarmness in contrast to their focus and passion. How can we cultivate the deep desire for the Lord that we see in these women from an era long ago? What must we do to uncover the same spiritual yearning that the Beguines experienced?

We begin by acknowledging the distracted state of our inner lives. Taking an honest look at our disordered desires, we face the many things that pull on and clamor for our attention and affection. When we examine how we use our time and focus our attention, we realize how disordered our priorities are and how disoriented our hearts have become. As we recognize the warped state of our desires and wishes, we begin to surrender them to the Lord one by one. Some things we crave may be good in and of themselves, but they must take a proper place in our lives. Others may in fact be idols that we need to renounce and discard.

Then we can allow the deep longing in our hearts to surface— we can dare to desire. How often we are afraid to tap into our subterranean desires because we know we might be disappointed. Will we be hurt if we open our hearts? What if our longing for love is not fulfilled? What if we surrender our hearts to intense longing for Jesus only to find that we cannot truly experience an intimate relationship with him as we had hoped?

Love requires risk. When we yield ourselves to be loved, it exposes us to potential hurt, and most of us avoid such a position of weakness. A true relationship makes us vulnerable because relationships are never static. Our emotions are bound to go up and down. These highs and lows are true even in our relationship with the Lord. At times we cannot seem to connect with him. Other times he surprises us with his manifest presence. Vital Christianity entails vulnerability.

The three women authors included in this volume—Beatrice, Hadewijch and Mechthild—all recognize that we can be hurt or disappointed in our love relationship with the Lord. Because it is truly a love affair with another person, we are vulnerable to pain, and their words describe the terrible ache they feel when God's presence seems to disappear. Beatrice depicts this inner ache under the rubric of love's various modes; Hadewijch discusses it in terms of spiritual sweetness. Despite the danger of being hurt, all the Beguines challenge us to open up to the Lord.

In one of her poems Hadewijch calls us as her readers to take the adventure of love. Although we might feel pain at times, in the long run we will discover God's great faithfulness to us. If we persevere, we will experience the fidelity of divine love:

> Love always rewards, even though she comes late.
>> Those who forsake themselves for her,
> And follow her highest counsel,
> And remain steadfast in longing,
>> She shall compensate with love.[9]

So we must nurture the noble desires within. The more we delight in the Lord, the purer will be our hearts' orientation. Psalm 37:4 states, "Delight yourself in the Lord and he will give you the desires of your heart." The more our lives center about the Lord, the more our attractions will be the right ones. He will give us desires that are in agreement with himself and his character. Although he often seems to be late in filling his promises to us, the Lord is always faithful and will fulfill the genuine desires of our hearts. Like the Beguines, we can dare to fan into flame the good desires of our hearts.

PRACTICE SOAKING IN GOD'S WORD

For most Beguines, the entire day was organized around Scripture. Their medieval practice of *lectio divina* offers much to busy Christians today. Most of us are not able to work in silence throughout the day as they did; however, we should not therefore dismiss their model of devotion. If we desire to cultivate God's presence in our lives and nurture his Word in our hearts, we can approximate their experience. By cultivating the four rhythms of *lectio divina* in our lives, we can savor Scripture and steep our thoughts in God's Word all day long.

The first rhythm, *lectio,* is to take a passage of the Bible and read it several times. Here we focus on a brief passage—perhaps a portion of a chapter from one of the Gospels—and pore over it carefully. Reading out loud is best because it slows us down, enables us to hear Scripture with our ears and alerts us to key terms and insights we might otherwise overlook. When we pronounce the words we taste God's Word, which is "sweeter than honey" (Psalm 19:10), savoring each syllable we speak. As we repeat the passage several times we notice small but important pieces that we missed the first time through. "Rather than rushing on to the next chapter so that we can complete a reading or study assignment," asserts spiritual director Ruth Haley Barton, "we stay in the place where God is speaking to us."[10]

When we close our Bible, our time in God's Word is not finished for the day but rather just beginning. As the Beguines did, we can saturate our thoughts as we practice the second rhythm of *meditatio.* Here we reflect on what we have read, pondering the passage and picturing it in our minds. We imagine the events, see the sun sparkle on the waves of the Sea of Galilee, smell the fish and feel the spray off the lake. We mentally place ourselves into that setting and watch Jesus perform miracle after miracle. Perhaps we memorize some verses so that we can carry them with us all day. Periodically we review the passage and allow God's Word to infuse our whole consciousness. In short, we soak in the Scripture and allow it to drench our minds, our hearts and our lives as the Lord commands in Joshua 1:8: "Do not let this Book of the Law depart from your mouth; meditate on it day and night, so that you may be careful to do everything written in it."

We should pay special attention to verses that arrest our attention, even if at the moment we are not sure why. On the one hand, notes Robert Mulholland in his book *Shaped by the Word*, the Holy Spirit highlights verses that bring comfort to places where we are fearful and crying out for peace. On the other hand, we are troubled by verses that confront our complacency and call us out of lukewarmness, apathy or self-centeredness. We must listen carefully and respond courageously, pulling down our defenses and allowing God's Word to convict us and perform surgery on our hearts, cutting away all that is not right. God breaks into our world in both conviction and encouragement. As Mulholland notes, "Transformation occurs when scripture is viewed as a place of encounter with God that is approached by yielding the false self and its agenda, by opening one's self unconditionally to God, and by a hunger to respond in love to whatever God desires."[11]

Meditation on Scripture leads naturally into *oratio*, the third rhythm of prayer. As our hearts and minds are saturated with God's thoughts we spontaneously begin to pray those thoughts back to him. Here we ask God the difficult questions that must be addressed: What are you exposing in my life—attitudes, words or actions? Where am I clinging to something I need to release? What do I fear? How must I change? Throughout the day we find ourselves petitioning: Develop in me the perseverance described in this passage. Soften my heart as you did Zacchaeus's. Give me boldness like the Canaanite woman who approached Jesus. So often today we detach our Bible reading from our prayer. We read Scripture rapidly to gain information and then fly through our shopping list of prayer requests, failing to meditate at any point. *Lectio divina* works in the opposite manner, allowing time and space for our hearts to become fully engaged in God's Word.

After responding in prayer, the fourth rhythm is to rest in God's presence in *contemplatio*. Like allowing a piece of good chocolate to melt on our tongue, we relish what the Lord has spoken to us through Scripture and we enjoy his company. Whether we remain quietly in a chair before leaving our devotional time or rise to take a walk with the Lord, we resist the temptation to rush into the day's activities. Adoring, listening and enjoying are the operative functions at this time. Like two lovers sitting on a swing together or strolling hand in hand, we delight in Jesus' closeness to us. No words need to be spoken. Here we do not attempt to learn something new but simply appreciate God's nearness and bask in his love. We take time to stand in silent awe of the Lord as described in Psalm 27:4: "to gaze upon the beauty of the LORD and to seek him in his temple." In this verse, *contemplatio* is the Latin term employed for "gazing upon" or "beholding" the Lord. Sometimes our contemplation in his presence is brief; other times we maintain our focus for a longer period. In either case we cultivate the relational side of our faith as we simply keep company with our God.

While these four rhythms are progressive, moving from the reading of Scripture to meditating on it to praying the passage over our lives to attending to God's presence, in practice we find that we often flow back and forth among these various elements. After praying the passage, we might return to meditate on it further and then glide back into more prayer. The rhythms of *lectio divina* are not so much a method but a mindset—an attitude of receptivity—toward God's Word.

RECOLLECTING OURSELVES

Like untold numbers of Beguines through the centuries, when we practice prayer, Scripture reading and contemplation, we move toward a life that is recollected. And recollection is necessary to live a God-hued life.

Recollection is a classic term referring to the intentional "recollecting" of our scattered thoughts and the reestablishment of our focus on our true inner desire. Here we reorient our distracted attention and reorder our divided affections. We pull back from the "muchness" and "manyness" of our preoccupied existence in order to attend to Jesus' presence within—a presence that brings wholeness to our fragmentation, integrity to our brokenness and oneness to our disintegrated way of being. We face those things that have sidetracked us in order to center ourselves afresh on the one thing: literally the One who fashioned us in his image and always holds our best interest in mind. As we regather our thoughts, our inner lives are healed. As we recollect our focus throughout the day, our perspectives change. Through inner recollection we cultivate a deeper spiritual life.

Before we can recollect ourselves for the whole day, we must do so for shorter amounts of time. We must learn to still ourselves in dedicated times of solitude with God. "Without solitude it is virtually impossible to live a spiritual life," asserts Henri Nouwen, renowned author on spiritual formation. "Solitude begins with a time and place for God, and him alone. If we really believe not only that God exists but also that he is actively present in our lives—healing, teaching, and guiding—we need to set aside a time and space to give him our undivided attention."[12] In this solitary place we are invited into a vital relationship with Jesus. Here we share our pressing needs and our secret dreams. We listen for the voice of his love, acceptance and forgiveness. In prayer we likewise bring those around us into the Almighty's presence in order to see him touch their lives with his fathomless mercy.

While the pursuit of deep devotion can tempt people to pull away from the world and live a secluded existence of solitude and perpetual contemplation, most of us are called to the active life. This does not mean we abandon intentional times of recollection, however. In fact, these times are what empower us to be in the world but not of it. Solitude is essential if we hope to re-gather the fragmented pieces of our lives and usher them into God's presence. From silence and stillness we reemerge to our daily responsibilities with a restored focus and fresh perspective, and we re-engage the dynamic world around us with newfound freedom.

The Beguines model for us a recollected life. They hand down a paradigm for devotion to God's Word that provides us a picture of what a day centered about Scripture can look like. They call us to nurture a life of prayer and give us courage to cultivate the deep desires of our heart. Ultimately the Beguines give us hope that, as we simplify our existence, we will be free to attend to God's powerful presence in our lives.

Personal Response
Drinking from Springs of Living Water

Reflection and Journaling

What are the deepest desires of your heart? In what ways are they directed toward genuine fulfillment in God? In what ways have you instead settled for passing wants, temporal pleasures or blaring demands in life?

How do you hope to cultivate your life of prayer? How do you long for more time alone with God? In what practical ways can you foster recollection in your life this week? Where can you go to ensure your times of solitude will not be interrupted?

What is going well in your Bible reading and what would you like to improve? How can the model employed by medieval believers bring fresh energy for you to soak in God's Word? Which rhythms of *lectio divina* would you like to give special attention to?

Scripture

Read Psalm 37 out loud. What are some fresh ways you can actively delight yourself in the Lord? How can you hope in him and wait on him this week?

Over the coming week, work your way through Psalm 119. In your journal or on a sheet of paper write down all the words describing the psalmist's love for God's Word. Then record the ways his Word leads us, directs us and corrects us.

Creativity and Action

Express your longing for God's felt presence in your life. You could write a prayer to the Lord or pen your thoughts in a poem. Perhaps you could express the yearning of your heart better in art work or dance. What does that inner yearning feel like? How do you express it to God? How does the divine presence manifest itself to you?

Community

Share with a close friend some areas where your thoughts, your character and your actions are least like Christ's. Take time to pray together and invite the Lord to transform these facets of your life.

Consider establishing a community Scripture reading with members of your household or a close friend. If you cannot meet daily, perhaps you can get together once a week to read the Bible aloud.

4

Seasons of the Soul

Beatrice of Nazareth Explores
Modes of Loving God

As the deer pants for streams of water,
so my soul pants for you, O God. . . .
Why are you downcast, O my soul?
Why so disturbed within me?
Put your hope in God,
for I will yet praise him,
my Savior and my God.

PSALM 42:1, 5

[God's] love passes through the senses and storms the soul with all its might. All the while that love grows in the soul, it ascends to God longingly and, richly flowing, opens up to receive the wonder that is approaching. It dissolves through the soul into the senses.

MECHTHILD OF MAGDEBURG

LOVE IS STORMY. Some seasons of relationship pulsate with fresh-ness and hope. Others fill our hearts with longing and disturb our souls within us. Yet in a lasting relationship, tumultuous times eventually give way to new seasons of enjoyment and delight.

We observe these seasons of love when we watch young people

enter into relationship. The first season is falling in love. The couple longs for deeper friendship and hopes that this may be "the one." She thinks of him every waking moment. He simply acts goofy. As the couple matures, infatuated feelings morph into active love. They realize that genuine love must express itself in action. Less focused on their emotions, they turn their attention to serving one another. He drives across town to paint her apartment, and she proofreads his term paper. He buys a gift to commemorate six months of dating, and she offers a place for his sister to stay during a weekend visit.

If the relationship continues, the couple becomes engaged. Their love turns red-hot. This is the stage of fiery love—the couple cannot get enough of each other. As marriage approaches, they want more time together, more tenderness and more touch. The sweet feelings of earlier days transition into a tormented love that will not be satisfied.

Finally the wedding day comes! At last their longing is consummated. As the two become one, the relationship emerges onto a whole new plane. They enjoy the overwhelming joys of love and intimacy they have yearned for so long.

This is the point when movies end but where life together begins in earnest. As married existence settles into everyday life, both the man and the woman begin to long again. When that longing is properly channeled, it provides the impetus to build an enduring marriage. It energizes the daily toil of maintaining job and home. It sustains them through disagreements and difficult times. That longing ultimately brings them back together, closer than before. The sparks of love are rekindled.

God is truly a personal being who welcomes us to experience and explore a genuine bond with him. Not a distant deity or some divine abstraction, God exists eternally as three persons in loving communion with each other. Such a God must be encountered on a relational level. As frail and sometimes fickle human beings, we experience relationship with the Lord with fluctuating emotions, as the Psalms well illustrate. The contours of our friendship with God develop and change. Such dynamics are to be expected.

From the first blush of falling in love with Jesus through long years that test our commitment, relationship with the Lord traverses various seasons of the soul. During these seasons our love expresses itself in sundry ways. It sees the flame of faith burn brightly in the springtime of our walk with Christ, and it rekindles that spark of love when the initial fires die down. Its intensity ebbs and flows, yet it remains one relationship.

Recognizing these diverse seasons, these various manifestations of our friendship with the Lord, helps us to negotiate the twists and turns common to Christian experience. We begin to understand the shifts that take place within our hearts, and we become more patient with believers around us who are experiencing a very different season of love.

BEATRICE: ON SEVEN MANNERS OF HOLY LOVE

One of the most insightful explorations of our love relationship with God was written by a woman of the thirteen-century revival named Beatrice of Nazareth. Her mother passed away when Beatrice was six, so her father sent her to a household of Beguines to receive a good education, training in Christian character and motherly love. In time Beatrice joined a Cistercian convent and guided many young women in their personal walk with Christ.

Most of what we know about Beatrice's life comes from her *Vita*—"Life"—the spiritual biography written by the chaplain of the convent in Nazareth.[1] While the *Vita* is based on Beatrice's journal, her original writings have been lost except for one booklet titled *On Seven Manners of Holy Love*. Writing in Dutch, Beatrice described seven ways we experience being in love with Christ. In this brief work she explores various facets of a believer's relationship with the Lord using the categories of love poetry common to her day. Just as we encounter different dynamics of love and progress along various steps of a romantic relationship, so we experience diverse modes of love in our relationship with Christ.

Beatrice employs these seven manners of love to portray our progress in spiritual formation. New believers begin with an insatiable inner hunger. Just as babies yearn for milk, new Christians will naturally long for the Lord. Over the years, that longing develops into service. If we are emotionally healthy, we will enthusiastically desire to serve those around us. These modes continue to build on each other. As we move from one to the next, however, we never completely abandon the earlier dynamics of love; rather, we see that these modes overlap and flow into each other as we move toward maturity.[2]

Although it is brief, *On Seven Manners of Holy Love* is a gold mine of spiritual insight in which the author sheds light on the process of Christian growth. Beatrice was one of the first women to examine the themes of spiritual love in writing, as well as one of the first authors in northern Europe to write about spiritual formation in the vernacular rather than Latin.[3] Using language that plucks our heartstrings, Beatrice sensitively expresses both the joys and the pains that we go through as we progress in our lifelong journey with the Lord.

Through her work Beatrice invites us to join her in following our hearts' desire for Christ. She mentors us as her readers as we progress in the spiritual life. Because she is unafraid to face the struggles we meet along the way, this godly woman helps prepare us for the difficult passages in our own pilgrimage. She encourages us in those stormy times and always assures us that the journey is worthwhile as we enter ever-deeper realms of love for Jesus our Savior.

FIRST MODE: LONGING LOVE

The first mode of love in the Christian life is longing love. Such yearning for the Lord is "surely a longing arising from love," writes

Beatrice: "that is, the pious soul desiring to serve our Lord faithfully, to follow him vigorously and to love him truly."[4] Our deep desire for the Lord draws us to him initially and floods our hearts as we grow in knowledge of him. Such yearning energizes us throughout the entirety of our Christian experience. According to Beatrice it is love, not fear, that truly motivates the believer's relationship with the Lord.

In this first mode—first stage—of love we set aside our carnal cravings and press toward an intimate relationship with Jesus. Out of holy desire we place Christ at the center of our heart and remove all pretenders to his throne. This mode is "an active longing," states Beatrice. "It must rule a long time in the heart before it can thoroughly expel all opposition."[5]

Ultimately we yearn to regain the original relationship Adam and Eve enjoyed with God in the Garden of Eden. This is the friendship the Lord always intended us to have with him, and he desires to restore us to the divine image and likeness we had at creation. In short, he not only wants to forgive us but also to conform us to the likeness of Christ. The more we are transformed, the more of God's love we are able to partake. But that transformation begins with the hard work of facing ourselves honestly.

Self-knowledge is the realization of our hidden thoughts, selfish motivations and less-than-godly actions. The soul that truly longs for the Lord, exhorts Beatrice, "often seriously scrutinizes what it is, what it should be . . . and what is lacking to its desire. With all its diligence, with great longing . . . it strives to beware [of] and avoid whatever can impede or harm it in this matter."[6] The soul that truly longs for the Lord, she asserts, must regularly take a candid look at itself. Being conformed to the divine image is a painful process, but it is one we yearn for deep inside because we desire to be ever closer to our Savior.

For Beatrice, spiritual growth has more to do with a passionate pursuit of Christ than the practice of any ascetic discipline. While she recognizes the role of self-denial and the painful process of growing in self-knowledge, it is our ardor for Jesus and the experience of his love that draw us onward in our Christian journey.

In our day we can experience the same spiritual season of new love that Beatrice describes. Entering a personal relationship with Jesus ignites the feelings of falling in love. Constantly we think about this wonderful new Friend, and we talk continually about the joy he has brought to our lives. Numerous worship choruses reflect this fresh first love for the Lord, and, not surprising, young believers resonate with these lyrics and sing them with passion.

Love, however, does not remain in eternal springtime. As older believers well know, it moves on to other seasons that test our resolve and deepen our commitment. Thus Beatrice continues her exploration of holy love.

SECOND MODE: LOVING SERVICE WITHOUT MEASURE

The second mode of loving God is through service. When we have come into a vital relationship with the Lord, we want above all else to serve him. Because we adore Jesus, we wish to attend to him with every ounce of our strength, and we are willing to labor in any and every way at our disposal. This service is not motivated by an attempt to earn something but by our undivided devotion to him. In this second manner of love, our soul "sets itself the task to serve our Lord freely out of love alone, without any other motive and without any reward of grace or glory . . . [serving] lovingly, without measure, beyond measure and beyond human sense and reason, faithfully performing every service."[7]

Such an attitude of service is seen when two people in love attempt to please each other in any way possible. They wait on the other one and are glad to perform the most menial tasks. So too do we become passionate to serve the Lord as we mature in him. Nothing seems too difficult. Interruptions and difficulties that would otherwise irritate us pass unnoticed. Beatrice writes:

When the soul attains this state, it becomes so ardent in desire, so ready to serve, so nimble in work, so meek in annoyance, so joyful in trouble! With its whole being it desires to please the Lord, and it is pleasant for it to find something to do or to suffer for the service and honor of love.[8]

A clear sign that we are growing in Christ is that we begin to ask how we can serve him. We desire to assist him in any way possible, and one of the foremost ways we display our love is to minister to others. Without such service our faith becomes narcissistic. But because we are in relationship with the Lord, our focus is on him and no longer on our own interests. In fact, we forget about ourselves when we are busily engaged in labor for the One we love. We serve Jesus not for our own benefit but as a gift. Work seems effortless. Because all that we do springs from love, even adversity seems light to us in this season of life.

Teaching at a Christian college, I have the opportunity to watch many young believers transition into this stage of service. It is exceptionally rewarding to see them catch on fire for the Lord. Some do street evangelism; others establish communities in the inner city to reach out to the homeless. Many embark on short-term mission trips, and some continue on to invest the remainder of their lives overseas. No task is too difficult and no ministry call too extreme. In fact, the more challenging the mission—and the more remote its location—the more excited they become to tackle the assignment!

THIRD MODE: THE TORMENT OF LOVE

Frustration arises, however, when we realize that we simply cannot do enough, notes Beatrice. We love the Lord and want to demonstrate our affection through our actions, but we find that no matter how much we accomplish, it cannot sufficiently express our gratitude. In our zeal for the Lord we adopt new spiritual disciplines and volunteer for every ministry that presents itself.

Beatrice observes how people in this mode work harder and longer but are never at peace: "Sometimes this desire so greatly agitates the soul that it strives vigorously to undertake everything, to follow after every virtue, to suffer and endure everything, to fulfill all its work in love, withholding nothing and without measure."[9]

We worship God and serve him with all of our strength, but the reality is that we are attempting the impossible. There is no way we can repay the Lord for what he has done for us. Although we know this mentally, we try anyway, and our effort causes us great unrest. "The soul well knows that fulfilling this desire much exceeds its own strength and human reason," Beatrice writes, "and yet it cannot moderate, contain or calm itself."[10]

As a result of our frustrated desire to fully express our love, we are disquieted to the point that all of life becomes a torment. Our soul in this stage "does what it can; it praises and thanks Love; it works and labors for Love; it desires and sighs for Love; it gives itself wholly to Love, and it perfects in love everything it does. [Nevertheless] all this gives the soul no rest."[11] We must simply endure the aggravation of this third mode of love until Christ comes to us anew and moves us into a fresh encounter of love.

FOURTH MODE: OVERWHELMED BY LOVE

In time the Lord ushers us into a new intimacy with himself, and we are overwhelmed by his presence. This is the fourth way we experience our love relationship with God. Beatrice describes this new manner of love thus:

> Sometimes it happens that love is sweetly awakened in the soul, rising up with joy, and flows in the heart without any human collaboration. And then the heart is so touched with tender love, is drawn towards love with such desire, is em-

braced so cordially by love, is subjected by love so strongly, and is held in love's embrace so lovingly, that it is wholly conquered by love.[12]

What a wonderful season of life this is! Although we have known cognitively that the Lord loves us, we now experience the reality of this divine embrace as never before. As we encounter God personally, our soul "feels a great closeness to God, a substantial clarity, a wonderful delight, a noble liberty and a ravishing sweetness," writes Beatrice. Our whole being is submerged in God's ocean of love and acceptance. Our soul "feels all its senses sanctified in love, its will turned into love and so deeply immersed and absorbed in the abyss of love that it is made wholly into love."[13]

Thus with great delight we experience the Lord's presence afresh. Here we enjoy such sweetness and pleasure that our soul is caught up into a new level of oneness with God. "Love's beauty has consumed it. Love's strength has eaten it up. Love's sweetness has immersed it. Love's greatness has absorbed it. Love's exaltedness has raised it up and so united it to itself that the soul must wholly belong to Love," says Beatrice. "When the soul feels itself in the superabundance of delights and in this great fullness of heart, its mind is wholly immersed in love and its body is withdrawn from itself; the heart melts away and all its power is consumed."[14] As we sink deep into God's mercy, our hearts melt, and we lose strength as we are raptured in the heights of divine love. Such sweet love gives us freedom and delight; here we are safe and secure in our intimacy with the Lord.

Over years of Christian service I have seen many people experience God's love in much the same way Beatrice describes. Far from being "mere emotionalism," such powerful encounters are often life-changing. Indeed, any experience must be tested by its fruit. If people are simply following their feelings, they will soon veer off into selfishness and sin. If, however, they have been

touched by the Lord, their lives will be transformed. Their intense
encounter with the Lord will lead them into a deeper love for God,
greater surrender to his will and stronger perseverance during difficult times.

FIFTH MODE: FRENZIED LOVE

The intense intimacy of the fourth mode erupts into the frenzied
desire of Beatrice's fifth mode. The closeness we have experienced
with the Lord makes us ravenous for more. Because we are still in
our mortal bodies, however, we cannot attain all that we desire.
This love is a violent love that yearns for further encounter with
the Lord. Because we cannot acquire enough of God, we become
aggravated and annoyed. We are dissatisfied with the affection we
have received and impatiently crave still more.

Such intensity hurts. In our passion for God we become wounded
in love. The storm rages within us and our heart becomes so frenzied we think it will drive us mad. Like others in her day, Beatrice
describes this feeling as if she were going to explode. At times her
soul is in such an uproar that she fears she is going crazy:

> So it seems that its veins are opened and its blood is boiling
> out, its marrow is withered and its legs are weak, its chest
> burns and its throat is dry, so that its face and all its mem-
> bers perceive the inner heat and experience the tumult that
> love is making. At this time she also feels an arrow piercing
> through her heart all the way to the throat and beyond, even
> to the brain, as if she would lose her mind.[15]

This stage is like the passionate love of two people who are about
to be married. In the weeks preceding their wedding day, they are
not able express their aching desire as they would like, and they
often become agitated, impatient and exhausted. Such is the obsession of love we may at times experience with the Lord. This powerful love is the antithesis of the lukewarmness of Christians who

have lost their first love. Although it is painful and frustrating beyond belief, the frenzied love of Beatrice's fifth mode is a committed love that desires the Lord beyond all measure or reason.

SIXTH MODE: BRIDAL INTIMACY

In time, the violent passion of the fifth mode gives way to a wonderful new season of relationship—experiencing ourselves as the bride of Christ. The storm passes and the clear sunlight of Jesus' love enfolds us. We know the highest state of union with the Lord that is possible in this lifetime as we enter the sixth manner of love: bridal intimacy. Such closeness is what we have desired all along, and we are now allowed to drink our fill of love.

When our soul, the bride, reaches this sixth state, "she feels that love has conquered all her adversaries within her, has corrected her defects and subdued her senses, has adorned her nature, has amplified and exalted her state of soul and gained dominion over herself."[16] Here we walk in self-control as never before, no longer dominated by our passions and feelings.

To prepare us for this stage, God uses the struggles along the way to strip us of our fleshy cravings, our catering to the senses and our self-will. Beatrice insists that all believers who truly desire to experience this loving intimacy must first pass through the tempest of the previous season. Those who want to reach this sixth mode cannot do so "if they spare themselves in great labors and many pains" during the previous stage.[17] We cannot skip a step. We cannot force the process. Like normal human development, our spiritual growth takes time and patience. There are no shortcuts to maturity.

Unlike earlier stages of the Christian life when we felt we always needed to be engaged in some form of ministry or service, we no longer work ourselves to exhaustion, trying to prove our commitment to the Lord. Our relationship with the Lord is not based on fear or on works. We are free to serve, but we are also free to rest.

Thus we enter into a comfortable relationship with God, whose love is our security and repose. "Like a fish swimming in a broad river and resting in the depths, and like a bird flying boldly in the vastness and the height of the sky, so the soul feels its spirit moving freely in the breadth and depth and vastness and height of love."[18]

Beatrice describes the soul in this state as the "lady" of the manor. Like a wife of many years, we become familiar with the Lord and comfortable with him. But as is true in marriage, such familiarity and rest come only after we have passed through some stormy years.

In this stage, asserts Beatrice, we are finally in full relationship with God. Our souls have been restored to his image and likeness, as they were originally created to be. Obedience comes easily. We are free to do the things we ought and to avoid anything that would offend God. Here we enjoy "some hint of divine power and clear purity and spiritual sweetness and desirable liberty, a discerning wisdom, a gentle drawing near to our Lord and an intimate knowledge of God."[19] In such intimacy we find the fulfillment of our souls' deepest desire.

SEVENTH MODE: RENEWED LONGING

In time, however, fresh longings stir within us and our hearts begin to yearn for something new, something more, something we cannot even identify. Thus our pursuit of the Lord begins afresh. We feel as if we are falling in love with the Lord all over again, and we experience an intensity that we thought was gone forever.

So long as we are on earth we will continue to desire more of the Lord. We long to have our hearts completely fulfilled, but in this life they can never be fully satisfied. The pilgrimage of the believer is marked with seasons of renewed desire for the Lord, which will be satisfied in full only when we see him face to face. Although we have experienced various progressing modes of love along the way, the yearning is always at work in our hearts.

That longing makes sense because the Lord is infinite and incomprehensible. No matter how much we experience divine love, there is still more to know. We desire to be drawn into the eternity of God's love and unfathomable depths of his divine being. But we have hope: we look forward to the final consummation of our union with Christ in heaven. Beatrice assures us that in eternity we will be "united with [our] Bridegroom and will become one spirit with him in inseparable faithfulness and eternal love."[20]

SPIRITUAL DIRECTION FOR OUR LIVES

What can we learn from Beatrice's insightful little book *On Seven Manners of Holy Love?* First, for those who are young, Beatrice models a passionate faith. Unafraid to face the stirrings in her soul, she unabashedly falls in love with Jesus. Yet Beatrice keeps her focus on the Lord and acknowledges that inner fervor and feelings fluctuate over time. Such emphasis is important in our day because pop culture places such a high premium on emotions. Undirected and unbridled passions will ultimately lead us astray. Only as we channel our inner drives toward Jesus will we find any lasting fulfillment.

For those who have walked with the Lord over some years, Beatrice helps us to realize that we must all weather various storms of the soul. One season is characterized by tormented longing; another sees the realization of that inner desire. Many who read Beatrice's seven stages identify with her experience and receive insight and encouragement from her observations. Like this saintly thirteenth-century woman, we also can experience dramatic variation from one season to the next. Our emotions radiate every color of the rainbow. Life is never bland. When we are in love, we are fanatically in love. If we feel destitute, we are overwhelmed by our distress.

If, like Beatrice, the seasons of our life are painted in bold contrast, we can be encouraged—we are in good company! Rather than ignoring the changing phases in our life, we must learn to appreciate their rhythms, as Howard Macy terms them.[21] One way Christians have done this over the centuries is to saturate ourselves with the Psalms. When we are in a difficult period, we can remind ourselves that this will not last forever. As David states in Psalm 42:5,

> Why are you downcast, O my soul?
>   Why so disturbed within me?
> Put your hope in God,
>   for I will yet praise him.

Likewise, when everything seems wonderful, we must not delude ourselves into thinking that this phase will continue the remainder of our days. Life is a rhythm of storm and sunshine.

Some readers resonate fully with Beatrice's language of intimacy and emotional experience. Others express their walk with God in less affective language. Yet all believers desiring a personal connection with God can benefit from her insights and fascinating discussion of our multifaceted relationship with the Lord.

PILGRIMAGE OVER THE LONG HAUL

Following Christ over the long haul is easier said than done. When I was a college student I joined a Christian fellowship filled with friends on fire for the Lord. After graduation and marriage for most of us came the long years of middle life—earning a living, raising a family and taking care of a home. For many, zeal gave way to exhaustion. Intimacy with the Lord dissipated into a numb ache for something more. Some feared that they had somehow failed the Lord. Yet underneath remained a deep yearning to serve God and enjoy renewed intimacy with him. To such believers Beatrice offers tremendous hope. There is renewed longing and a fresh season of springtime ahead.

A lifelong spiritual journey calls for fortitude of character: following Christ has never been for the faint of heart. As a whole, Christians in our day have lost the secret of endurance; our instant-gratification culture has undermined any concept of long-term commitment. Even sermons from the pulpit often focus on a quick fix for immediate needs and fail to teach us how to foster a purposeful pursuit of Christ through the vicissitudes of life. Enduring faith, however, does not center on comforts or easily give up, but rather tenaciously presses forward despite challenging circumstances and inevitable discouragements.

Beatrice calls us to an enduring progress in the faith and reminds us that our pilgrimage is anything but static. We mature from infants in Christ to young men and women, finally to fathers and mothers of the faith (see 1 John 2:12-14). Our spiritual growth is a venture. From Augustine's *Confessions* to John Bunyan's *Pilgrim's Progress* to many contemporary works on the spiritual journey, Christians through the centuries have depicted the Christian life as a pilgrimage.

As *On Seven Manners of Holy Love* details, storms and droughts will come to us as well. Rather than evidence of backsliding, these are often signs that we are maturing and experiencing growing pains. Beatrice's insights offer encouragement and guidance as we, and those around us, press through troubling times into an ever-deeper intimacy with the Lord.

Personal Response
Drinking from Springs of Living Water

Reflection and Journaling

How would you describe your love relationship with Christ? How is it like or unlike a human romantic relationship?

Review Beatrice's seven manners of love. Which ones have you identified with at various seasons in your spiritual pilgrimage? Which mode do you resonate with right now?

In what ways are you longing for more of the Lord? What does that longing look like in your life right now? How are you currently pursuing that inner longing, or how are you ignoring it?

Scripture

Read Psalms 42 and 43. How does David give voice during a "down" season of his life? How is he able to encourage himself in the midst of that season?

Read 1 John 2:12-14. How does John refer to the progress of the Christian life from infant to mature adult? What characterizes the infant believer? The young man or woman in Christ? The mature father or mother in the faith?

Creativity and Action

If you are artistically inclined, express the current season of your soul with colored pencils or paint. Which color or colors will you choose? What scene best communicates your inner life right now? Where are you in the picture? Where is God?

Cultivate your relationship with the Lord this week by serving him as you minister to those around you. Who can you reach out to? How can you touch another life by some practical act of kindness?

Community

Share these various stages with one or two friends and ask them to reflect on their seasons of spiritual pilgrimage. Listen to their story and be attentive to both the joys and the pains of their heart.

5

Creative Community

The Beguines Model Spiritual Friendship

How good and pleasant it is
   when God's people live together in unity! . . .
It is as if the dew of Hermon
   were falling on Mount Zion.
For there the LORD bestows his blessing,
   even life forevermore.

PSALM 133:1-3 (TNIV)

No person in any situation can humble himself to better advantage than by
following Christian counsel with an obedient heart.

MECHTHILD OF MAGDEBURG

CHRISTIANS TODAY ARE SEEKING COMMUNITY. Our need to connect with others is inextricably woven together with our longing for intimacy with God.

The modern world obsession with the individual magnifies our need for meaningful friendship. Our society demands individual rights. We seek to climb the ladder of success and make a name for ourselves. We choose a lifestyle that caters to our comforts and entertainment. We worry about our health and obsess about our image. All in all, contemporary culture militates against genuine community.

This individualism colors our walk of faith more than most Christians care to admit. With few exceptions, spirituality today focuses on the isolated soul. Oblivious to the central role of friendship, we base our concept of inner growth on privately practiced spiritual disciplines. We envision Christian maturity as a solo race and approach spiritual formation as we would any area of self-betterment, such as going on a diet or exercising at the gym. We buy self-help manuals to guide us along paths of self-improvement and achieve a sense of self-fulfillment. While this workout ethic may keep us in physical shape, it offers but a shadow of inner transformation.

Exacerbating the situation, many of our churches—despite the word *community* in their names—lack the kinship that was familiar two generations ago. Church programs provide ample activity and stimulating entertainment, but they often fail to cultivate substantive connection. Seldom do we encourage young, middle-aged and older believers to share life and faith together on a meaningful plane. In an era when family life is eroding, holistic community is more important than ever. The younger generation can benefit from the time, attention and wisdom of seniors. In return, youth can offer their energy and idealism, along with a needed helping hand, to their elders. Yet by and large churches fail to facilitate such intergenerational friendships.

BEGUINE COMMUNITIES
Diametrically opposed to the individualism of today, the Beguines set an example of Christian life in community. They recognized the role other believers played in their spiritual progress and linked arms with like-minded believers along their pilgrimage. Although beguinages provided ample space for each woman to savor time alone with God, such solitude was set in the context of vibrant community life.

Part of the Beguine movement's success was the way it brought together women of all ages. Many Beguine communities consisted of separate homes built side by side, along the lines of the typical townhomes that lined the cobblestone streets of the time. Often a group of three or four women—perhaps relatives or close friends— would join the beguinage together and build such a townhome for themselves. Although some wealthier women owned their own townhomes, most houses served as communities in miniature.

Each home featured a walled-off garden so the women could grow vegetables. The house itself consisted of a common room, kitchen and several bedrooms, with each woman generally able to work with her hands in her own bedroom throughout the day. Beguines remained in possession of their property, a privilege highly regarded by the middle class families from which many of them came. However, when they died, their townhome passed on to the beguinage as a whole.

These Beguine townhomes were ordered around a commons or central courtyard. For this reason the larger compounds were referred to as "court beguinages"—*Begijnhoven* in Dutch. These common areas provided additional space for the women to grow crops. Some central courtyards were modest in size, surrounded by just a few dozen small townhomes, but most covered a plot of land the size of several football fields, with a hundred or more homes circling the perimeter. This layout with its open commons both reflected and contributed to the Beguines' community life.

Usually beguinages were built within city walls. After 1230, Beguine complexes became sizable, taking up whole sections of town. The *Begijnhoven* were walled off for the protection of the sisters. As these communities emerged, single and widowed Beguines who had been living scattered throughout the towns moved to live in common with others. When there was no room within the city, Beguine compounds were erected on the edge of town, annexing themselves to the city wall. This location also gave them access to the local stream, a necessary source of water for dying cloth and performing other functions of the textile trade in which many of the women were employed.

Soon the larger beguinages established their own parishes separate from the local priests and parishes in those cities. Church buildings were constructed in the center of the Beguine complex, usually on the large open courtyard. Many of these sanctuaries held several hundred women and were filled to capacity in their day. It should be noted that most of the cities of the day claimed only five thousand to twenty thousand inhabitants. Thus the Beguine congregations constituted a notable segment of their respective cities.

In time poorer single women from the surrounding villages moved to the cities to find employment. Because these newcomers could not afford to buy their own homes in the beguinage, they were provided beds in dormitory-style rooms in one of the Beguine houses. Here they found a safe place to live and grow spiritually. Most earned a modest living by working in the textile industry, which enabled them to pay rent and buy food. Even with such assistance, some women from the countryside could not afford to buy staples, so the Beguines established a food pantry or soup kitchen, referred to as the "Holy Ghost Table," a place where the poorest sisters could receive a free meal.

The Beguines evangelized the townspeople living around them, inviting other women to join them and experience the same personal relationship with the Lord that they enjoyed. Because they had contact with outsiders through teaching school, serving as nannies and working in the textile trade, they were able to influence many other women. The great growth of the Beguine movement in the mid-thirteenth century was due in part to the women's constant witness to others. They were passionately committed to Christ and welcomed other women into a transforming relationship with their Lord.

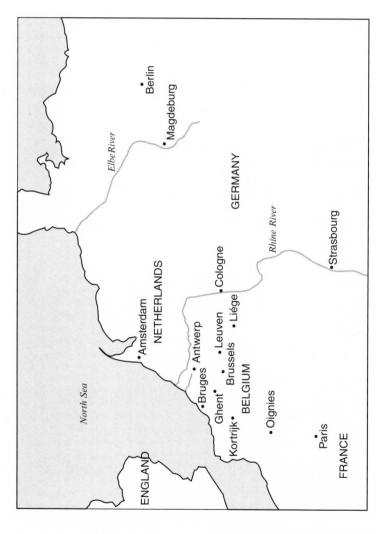

Northern Europe

Beguinage in Bruges.

Beguinage in Bruges.

Today one can get a taste of Beguine devotion by spending a day at the beguinage in the beautiful city of Bruges. Visitors are welcome in the back of the church while nuns hold chapel services for the daily office at various hours of the morning, afternoon and evening. Here one gains a sense of the common life and spirituality of the thousands of Beguines who once lived in northern Europe. In 1927, after the Beguines had died away, Benedictine nuns assumed the property. They wanted to carry on the tradition of the

Beguinage in Leuven.

Beguinage in Leuven.

Beguine movement, so today they wear the Beguine habit. Because this is an active cloister, visitors can experience grounds that have been set apart for prayer, quiet and meditation.

The complex in Leuven (Louvain in French) no longer houses Beguines but is part of the University of Leuven. Students and faculty live in the small townhomes and walk the narrow cobblestone streets on their way to class. The church building, dedicated to John the Baptist, still stands, and one can ob-

Bedroom in Bruges.

serve the foundation stone stating that its construction was begun in 1234. While most of the brick buildings were built in the sixteenth century, a few structures date from the earlier times of the Beguines, especially the infirmary, which is believed to have been established early in the thirteenth century.[a]

---

[a]See the booklet by Rik Uytterhoeven, *The Groot Begijnhof of Leuven,* trans. Guido Latré (Leuven, Belgium: Leuven University Press, 2000). In my conversation with him, Mr. Uytterhoeven noted that architects believe the infirmary is the original construction from the early thirteenth century.

Photo credits: Glenn E. Myers

Bedroom in Kortrijk.

OVERSIGHT AND PASTORAL CARE

Each Beguine community was self-governing. The smaller dormitory houses were overseen by a mistress or mother superior who directed the home's affairs and mentored the younger sisters. The larger *Begijnhoven* communities, which often included convents as well as hundreds of individual homes, were governed by a headmistress—*la grande dame*—along with several other mistresses who served as "elders." The headmistress often received counsel in both spiritual and practical matters from a local Dominican or Franciscan friar.

Important decisions, such as the appointment of a priest for the Beguine parish, were made jointly by the headmistress, the friar and the elder women. The parish priest for the Beguine complex, who lived just outside the walls, conducted church services and provided spiritual direction for the community. In some of the larger Beguine complexes, the priest had one or more assistants who aided him in teaching and guiding the large number of women.

Within Beguine communities, younger believers found older women to mentor them. Discipleship and spiritual direction were woven into the very fabric of community life. In addition to fellowship and financial assistance, the younger women also received basic schooling. They were guided in Christian character by the more mature sisters of the convent and received moral oversight from the house mistress. James of Vitry writes, "Led by one of them who surpasses the others in virtue and prudence, they receive instruction in good morals and in letters, and are trained in [spiritual] exercises, in manual labor and poverty, in denial of the self and humility."[1]

Accountability and confession were important dynamics of the Beguines' spiritual growth. At times the Beguine mistress served as confessor; at other times the priest or a visiting friar heard confessions. Those occasions in which women unburdened their souls provided the same kind of support that spiritual direction and small care groups do today. Women could divest their minds not only of sins but also of life's concerns; they looked forward to these opportunities to share their hearts.

LAY COMMUNITIES

Of particular interest to many contemporary readers is the fact that the Beguine communities attempted to bridge the gap between lay-people and the "religious," as monks and nuns were referred to. For hundreds of years before this, the primary way to pursue spiritual formation was to join a religious order and live under monastic rule. Beginning in the twelfth century, however, that situation changed. Beguines and other laypeople, mostly from the emerging middle class, were pursuing spiritual growth. Able to read and write in the vernacular, they obtained translations of the Bible as well as devotional works being written for the first time in Europe's common languages. Thus, forming their semimonastic communities, Beguines forged a middle way between the lifestyle of the religious and the majority of Christians who lived in the "world."

The Beguines were not the first or only group to cross this chasm. Various movements of laymen and laywomen in late medieval Europe were experimenting with similar structures, among them the Humiliati in Italy and the "Third Order" Franciscans and Dominicans. In fact, many Beghards—the smaller men's movement corresponding to the Beguines—eventually joined the Third Order Franciscans.[2]

Crossover between the Beguines and the nuns took place more often than one might expect. Beatrice of Nazareth, for example, was schooled by the Beguines before she entered the Cistercian order. Mechthild of Magdeburg lived as a Beguine most of her life but then joined the Benedictine convent at Helfta for the last decade of her life. While Beguines originally wore a plain dress as their uniform, over time their attire became more like the habits worn by nuns. Also, because of property issues, many Beguine convents, especially those in Germany, eventually united with the Dominican order. Whether nuns or Beguines, these thousands of women pursued a deeper relationship with Christ, and spiritual growth was always foremost in their mind.

Then as now, society did not know how to view these communities. They did not belong entirely under the religious umbrella because they were not accountable to an established order. But neither did they live the traditional family lives of most laity. Especially in late medieval Europe, such middle ground between lay and religious posed difficulties. Should community members come under the jurisdiction of the city or of church hierarchy? Such ambiguity contributed to the persecution that arose against the Beguines by the end of the thirteenth century. Nevertheless, the Beguines pursued their life in common and the spiritual growth it afforded them.

COMMUNITY FOR CONTEMPORARY CHRISTIANS

As believers our relationship with God must be personal, but it is not meant to be private. Christian community contributes to our Christian growth in vital ways. Community serves as the context for spiritual friendships to develop, offering a safe haven in which we are known by others and loved in the midst of our brokenness. Close believers in community model Christian character for us. Much of the Christian life is more caught than taught, and our lives can be permanently altered by watching others demonstrate godly disciplines, patient attitudes and genuine forgiveness. Friends in community encourage us when the spiritual journey seems long and circuitous. Their encouragement, instruction and input prod us forward in Christ.

The Beguines offer a wonderful model for believers today and welcome us to explore the possibility of community. So much of our contemporary focus is on "Jesus and me" that we tend to forget the relational dynamics of faith. The reality is that much of our significant growth as believers takes place through our interaction with others. We must take a serious look at the Beguines' model—and the gentle nudge it provides—to move beyond our individualistic concepts of spiritual formation.

Numerous Christian groups today are experimenting with community, much as the Beguines did in their day. This community can take many forms. Full-scale communal living is one option, and one that is being explored afresh, especially by the younger generation. Households comprising both single people and married couples are emerging in the inner city. Sometimes referred to as "New Monastics," believers in these communities pursue both spiritual growth and social action in some of the neediest neighborhoods.

One such community is The Simple Way, a group of believers living in a rundown neighborhood of north Philadelphia. Founded by Shane Claiborne, this communal group resides in a row home—much like that of the Beguines. Members live among the poor and serve the homeless, arguably the neediest segment of society today. In his book *The Irresistible Revolution: Living as an Ordinary Radical*, Claiborne articulates the goals of the community: "We are trying to raise up an army, not simply of street activists but of lovers—a community of people who have fallen desperately in love with God and with suffering people, and who allow those relationships to disturb and transform them."[3]

Dwelling together under one roof or in one compound is only one of many ways that genuine Christian community manifests itself. Others today are creating community through strong home groups, cell groups or prayer groups. Sharing on a more intimate level in these smaller settings, members cultivate spiritual friendship that cannot develop in larger church gatherings.

For such a group to develop into a genuine community takes intentional time together. It is vital for members to meet each week to fellowship, pray and explore Scripture together. When they also have the opportunity to work, play and eat together, their lives are further knit with one another. When singles and families in such groups live in the same neighborhood, they can begin to approximate a common life. In our modern obsession with being efficient, we must not forget that "quality time together" emerges only out of plain old "time together."

True community requires that we be vulnerable in sharing the weaker parts of our lives. Vulnerability, however, cannot be forced. Hearts tend to open spontaneously when they find a safe place. Home groups and cell groups must cultivate that safe atmosphere. Sometimes in our zeal for spiritual growth we become too quick to correct, which almost always backfires. While correction and instruction are part of genuine Christian community, they must come in the context of care.

Another type of community develops when two like-minded believers cultivate spiritual companionship. In his classic *Spiritual Friendship*, Aelred of Rievaulx describes such a bond.[4] Two friends may do many activities together, but the relationship becomes a spiritual friendship only when they make intentional time to discuss their lives, discern God's movement and pray together. And when they do meet together in this way, they are not alone. As Aelred says, there is a Third present with them. In the midst of today's emphasis on professional spiritual directors, let us not forget the beauty of unadorned spiritual friendship!

FLAWED PEOPLE IN IMPERFECT COMMUNITY

Christian community also helps us grow in a way we might not intuitively recognize: it gives us the opportunity to realize our blind spots. Those who know us well are best able to point out the bad behavior and cancerous attitudes that we cannot, or will not, face on our own. Our spiritual friends can confront us—hopefully in a gentle manner—and correct our less-than-Christlike conduct. Likewise, Christian community enables us to learn to forgive others' shortcomings. "Bear with each other," commands Paul in Colossians 3:13, "and forgive whatever grievances you may have against one another. Forgive as the Lord forgave you."

Christian character comes at a price. If you have ever experienced true community, you realize that even passionate pilgrims are far from perfect. If you spiritually dance with others, you are sure to have your toes stepped on—and that is okay. Patience grows in our lives only when it is tested by people and circumstances that make us impatient. Forgiveness flourishes in our hearts through forgiving wrongs done to us, especially by those closest to us. We begin to realize our own bad attitudes as we learn to forbear the selfishness and judgmental attitudes of others. We often learn as much from bad role models as we do from good ones.

It is crucial to acknowledge that the perfect Christian community does not exist. It would be all too easy to paint a romantic picture of the Beguines as an ideal community, but the portrait would be unrealistic. The truth is that the Beguines confronted all of the challenges any community faces. Although genuine believers, these women were fallen human beings like us. The mistresses had to keep order and on occasion dismiss some of the young women. Hadewijch was forced out of the community she led. Those who preached in the Beguine households, such as Johannes Tauler in the fourteenth century, continually confronted petty jealousy, backbiting and dissent.[5]

It is important for us to recognize the reality of the Beguines' shortcomings so we do not attempt to establish a utopian community. If we do so, we are bound to see our naive hopes dashed, and we will be tempted to pull away from community into isolation. "The serious Christian, set down for the first time in a Christian community, is likely to bring with him a very definite idea of what Christian life together should be and to try to realize it," observes Dietrich Bonhoeffer. "But God speedily shatters such dreams."[6] Indeed, God must destroy those idealistic hopes if genuine community is to be experienced. True community acknowledges the brokenness of others and ourselves, it faces the challenges of such fallenness, and it moves forward in sober realism, appreciating the blessings of community and embracing the growth that others' faults can germinate in us.

SOLITUDE AND COMMUNITY

We frequently think of community and solitude as polar opposites. In addition we are told that "introverts" prefer to be alone, "extroverts" choose crowds, and these inclinations are simply the way God made us. The reality, however, is that spiritual well-being and healthy emotional development entail a hearty combination of both time alone and time together. "*Let him who cannot be alone beware of community,*" contends Bonhoeffer. "But the reverse is also true: *Let him who is not in community beware of being alone.*"[7]

In solitude we cultivate a close relationship with the triune God. Over the years we open up ever-deeper areas of our life, attitudes and hearts. As we risk revealing the places we secretly believe are unlovable, we come to realize that the Lord indeed loves us with an everlasting, all-encompassing love. Community then provides an opportunity to share the love God has given us with others. In the day-in and day-out of relating to those around us, though, we often find that we have not been as fully changed within as we had hoped. "If anyone says, 'I love God,' yet hates his brother, he is a liar," states the apostle John bluntly. "For anyone who does not love his brother, whom he has seen, cannot love God, whom he has not seen" (1 John 4:20).

The Beguines beautifully model this balance of solitude and community. On the one hand, they guarded time alone for each woman so she could cultivate her personal relationship with Christ. Many of the Beguines worked throughout the day in their own rooms where they could devote their thoughts and their hearts to Scripture and prayer. On the other hand, these women lived together in community where they could enjoy the support, encouragement and camaraderie of a common life. Attending chapel morning and evening, they shared a mutual spiritual life and enjoyed each others' presence.

TRANSFORMING FRIENDSHIP

Living together in community as the Beguines did does not guarantee spiritual friendship; however, it provides a matrix in which genuine friendship can be cultivated. Experiencing love in a healthy friendship enables us to profoundly receive God's love on a whole new level. The converse is also true: the more we encounter God's healing love, the more we are able to reach out to others. Friendship with others and friendship with God go hand in hand. Not only are they two sides of one coin, they dynamically feed one another.

True friendship is transforming. It allows others to get close enough to us to discover our dysfunctions, addictions and underlying hurt. As painful as this process is, we find that when the other person uncovers the real "us"—with all our selfishness and ugliness—he or she continues to love us. After they have slipped behind our well-constructed walls of defense and seen us raw and naked, they still want to be our friend. Such experience of love will transform us from the inside out.

The more we experience this genuine love in community, the more we are able to grasp God's love. Although as Christians we mentally know God loves us, we often do not experience that love. "A healing friendship opens us up to the possibility that we can also accept ourselves in all our woundedness," asserts James Houston, noted author on the spiritual life. "As we open ourselves up to such friends, we can be encouraged to begin opening ourselves up to God too. We begin to learn at an emotional level how profoundly God has accepted us in Christ, because his love for us is infinite. Then with a deeper acceptance still, we learn that in his acceptance of us, we can accept ourselves."[8]

Personal Response
Drinking from Springs of Living Water

Reflection and Journaling

What inspires you about the Beguines and their willingness to form communities? What aspects of the Beguines' model would you like to incorporate into your life?

Currently, who are your closest spiritual friends? How are those friendships transformative? In what ways have they exposed issues hidden in your life? How have you found yourself loved despite your faults?

How can you make yourself more open to receive input that addresses the blind spots in your life?

Scripture

Read the book of Ruth. What catches your attention? How did Naomi influence Ruth's life? What is the role of commitment and genuine friendship in this story?

Read Colossians 3. How is Christ's character being formed in you through your interaction with family, friends and work associates? Whom do you need to forbear as you walk in humility, gentleness and patience? Whom do you need to forgive right now in your life?

Creativity and Action

Who has been a spiritual mentor in your life? If you have had one or more mentors, thank the Lord for this tremendous gift. Also, take some time to write—either in a journal or a thank-you card—what they have imparted in your life.

If you have not had a mentor, or if it has been some years since you had such a person in your life, who might you ask to provide spiritual direction?

Community

What fellowship do you enjoy at this point in your Christian walk? How is it life-giving for you? In what ways are you longing for something more? How can you cultivate the community you are a part of?

How can you pass on what you have received from others in community? How might you serve by becoming a mentor in someone else's life?

6

Savoring Inner Sweetness

Hadewijch Gives Invaluable Wisdom on Spiritual Experience

Taste and see that the LORD is good.

PSALM 34:8

The loving soul wants Love wholly, without delay;
It wishes at all hours to delight in sweetness.

HADEWIJCH OF BRABANT

OH, THE SWEETNESS OF GOD'S LOVE! The young girl was overwhelmed by delight when at the age of ten she first experienced this spiritual sweetness. Flooded by a sense of God's love, she tasted and saw firsthand his goodness. Through this intense encounter she was drawn into an intimate lifelong relationship with the Lord.

The girl's name was Hadewijch, a fairly common name for her time. She lived in the mid-thirteenth century in the duchy of Brabant, part of present-day Belgium. For years she enjoyed personal encounters with the Lord and relished his presence. Her life was permanently changed by the Lord's touch—once she had experi-

enced it she had no interest in anything the world had to offer.
Forever spoiled for worldly pleasures, she spent the rest of her
days pursuing Christ.

When Hadewijch grew older she moved away from her family
to become a Beguine. As she built her life with the women in the
community, Hadewijch cultivated deep friendships. She recognized that holy relationships are essential for holy living. In her
letters we read of Sara, Emma, Margriet and one unnamed Beguine who was closest of all to Hadewijch. These young women
looked to her for spiritual direction, and she served as a godly
mentor for them. Always practical in her advice, she never tired of
calling her sister Beguines into an intimate walk with Jesus. She
challenged them to surrender their lives completely to the Lord
and to be engulfed by his love. She encouraged them to persevere
through the dry times when they could not feel his touch, trusting
that he would reward their faithfulness in due time.

As Hadewijch matured, her encounters of spiritual sweetness
became less frequent. After years of savoring these experiences,
she no longer felt the Lord's presence. Her heart was in anguish.
Like a lover longing for the return of her beloved, she suffered torment of heart as she waited for fresh encounters with God.

While her experience was bitter, Hadewijch refused to allow
her heart to become embittered. She decided that she must not
regret her radical commitment to God or renounce the beauty of
her earlier season of spiritual sweetness. Instead, Hadewijch
learned to persevere in her relationship with the Lord. She began
to recognize that feelings do not last forever. A sense of absence is
part of all genuine relationships and spiritual experiences come
and go; therefore, she dared not look to elated emotions lest those
same sentiments betray her.

As the sense of God's presence that she had enjoyed for years
diminished, Hadewijch discovered that the path to spiritual adulthood traverses many a dry time. She realized that attempting to

hold onto past experiences only hindered her from becoming fully grown in the Lord. Through loss of spiritual sweetness she learned to wrestle with God. Rather than becoming passive during her sense of the Almighty's absence, Hadewijch discovered that she needed to pursue him as never before.

One of the best-known Beguines and the most skilled of their writers, Hadewijch recorded both the joy of spiritual sweetness and the corresponding desolations Christians face when they do not experience those blissful emotions. Especially in her letters, she encouraged younger sisters to pursue spiritual intimacy while she prepared them for the day those intimate feelings would fade.

Although we are certain about very few details of this amazing woman's life, we know a tremendous amount about her inner journey, her spiritual experience, her growth, her struggle and her counsel to believers who desire to press on to maturity in the Lord.

SPIRITUAL SWEETNESS

God calls all believers to a personal encounter with himself. Although we might employ different terminology to describe it, most of us can recount wonderful experiences of God's love. As new believers most of us experience unprecedented peace and joy when we enter our newfound relationship with the Savior. We bask in God's abiding presence, feel his love flood our hearts and delight in a constant sense of divine comfort surrounding us. As we fall in love with Jesus, life brims with spiritual light and freedom. We enjoy dynamic spiritual growth. This is the springtime of our faith. Everything is fresh. Everything is sweet.

As we grow, we continue to savor the inner pleasure given to us by the Lord. Some of us experience spiritual sweetness in solitude. Those exceptional times give us strength to face the challenges of life and remind us of the Lord's unfailing faithfulness toward us. Many of us enjoy intimate times with him during worship. We are caught up in his glory as we sing praises to the Creator and magnify his great majesty. What a freeing experience it is to forget ourselves and our problems in order to be fully present to God and his eternal reality! Tranquility and calm enfold us as we delight in the divine embrace.

Others of us enjoy spiritual elation when we partake of the Lord's Supper. Here we commune with Christ, relishing intimacy with the One who loves us so much that he died on the cross to carry away our sins. Many of the women in the thirteenth-century revival experienced Jesus powerfully and personally during the Eucharist. It was at the Lord's Table that they felt him in a unique and healing way.[1]

Still others of us embrace spiritual sweetness when we saturate ourselves in God's Word. The ordinances of the Lord are "sweeter than honey, than honey from the comb," as David declares in Psalm 19:10. When we immerse ourselves in Scripture we find how loved we are. As we savor the Word in our mouths and let it melt on our tongue like honey, we take pleasure in the divine Speaker of that Word.

ESSENTIAL TO SPIRITUAL GROWTH

This theme of sweetness, our sense of the Lord's presence, is central to Hadewijch's personal experience and her writing. Throughout the centuries other Christian writers have referred to this type of encounter as "inner consolation"—the wonderful sense of comfort we receive from the Lord. Psalm 16:11 describes it:

> You will show me the path of life;
>   In Your presence is fullness of joy;
>   At Your right hand are pleasures forevermore. (NKJV)

Hadewijch depicts this early season in a believer's life as a time when

> the heavens are open, and the attributes of the great God appear in the hearts of his secret friends with pleasure, and

with sweetness, and with joy. Then the blissful soul is led into a spiritual inebriation, in which she must play and surrender herself according to the sweetness she feels from within. No one blames her for this; she is the child of God and is blissful.[2]

According to Hadewijch, this season of sacred springtime is indispensable to believers' spiritual development because it draws them away from temporal attachments. When they delight in God's presence, they are freed from the shallow gratification of the flesh.

We can indeed make bold to say:
"You are mine, Beloved, and I am yours!"
And we say this because pleasure moves us,
And [the sense of] enjoyment sets us free.[3]

Hadewijch further contends, "Love ever makes him taste her so sweetly that he forgets everything on earth."[4] Nothing of the created order compares with the joy of an intimate relationship with Christ.

SPRINGTIME FADES

Over time, however, experiences of spiritual sweetness fade. As our wise Beguine observes, many new believers appear to be radically in love with the Lord, enjoying all the ecstasy that accompanies such a season, yet when they face troubling experiences in life, their love grows cold. Fair-weather friends of Jesus, these souls fail to continue with the Lord during the difficult times of life. In fact, notes Hadewijch, sometimes it is those who have been the most emotional—who feel the most intense spiritual sweetness early in their relationship with the Lord—who prove to be the least reliable in the long run:

Virtues and not sweetness are the proof of love, for it sometimes happens that he who loves less feels more sweetness.

Love is not in each person according to what he feels, but according as he is grounded in virtue and rooted in charity (Ephesians 3:17). Sometimes desire for God is sweet but not wholly divine, for it wells up from the senses rather than from grace.[5]

Believers who place too much emphasis on the consolations do not fare well in the long haul of the Christian life. When the feelings fade, so also do these people's love and devotion to God. Clutching to sensations, notes Hadewijch, they are ultimately led astray:

For we discover in these souls that as long as sweetness endures in them, they are gentle and fruitful. But when the sweetness vanishes, their love goes too; and thus the depths of their being remain hard and unfruitful. . . . These are fainthearted folk; they are easily elated when all is sweet and distressed when anything is bitter. A small heavenly favor makes their heart exceedingly joyful, and a small sorrow exceedingly afflicts it.[6]

Therefore, she concludes, it is not powerful emotion but Christlike character that demonstrates the depth of our commitment. As the New Testament lists "love, joy, peace, patience, kindness, goodness, faithfulness, gentleness and self-control" (Galatians 5:22-23) as fruit of our walking by the Spirit, so Hadewijch asserted that these virtues demonstrate a genuine love for the Lord:

But they who wish to enjoy the Beloved here on earth,
And dance with feelings of delight,
And dwell in this with pleasure,
    I say to them in advance:
They must truly adorn themselves with virtues,
    Or the course of study is a loss to them.[7]

What then should be said about the emotional dynamics of love that many believers experience in their relationship with the

Lord? "If [we] are in consolation," asserts Hadewijch, "let it be as Love wills; if [we] are disconsolate, again as Love wills."[8] We must enjoy spiritual sweetness when it comes and remain faithful to God when it goes. There is nothing wrong with the wonderful feelings that accompany our intimate times with the Lord; we should savor those times and be thankful for them. Yet when such sweetness disappears, we must persevere in our relationship with God and leave the well-being of our souls in his hands.

Such counsel by Hadewijch is hard for us contemporary Christians to hear. Advertisers promise us that we can have it all. Sermons equate the abundant life with the American "good life." In a world obsessed with feelings and experiences, it is easy to assume that spiritual sweetness is one of our inalienable rights. However, Hadewijch warns what can happen to those who cling to emotional consolation.

WEANED FROM SEEKING PLEASURE

If we are not discerning, we ultimately pursue human pleasure when we think we are seeking God. Hadewijch notes that at times our tears can be manifestations of self-focus. We often cry simply because we do not get our own way; our self-will has been frustrated. "In desires for devotion, all souls err who are seeking anything other than God. For we must seek God and nothing else."[9]

When we begin to pursue an experience or sensation instead of God, we are soon led off course. "In seeking spiritual sweetness, people err greatly," continues Hadewijch, "for there is very much emotional attraction in it, whether toward God or toward men."[10] In other words, at times when we think we are experiencing God's presence, we are rather trying to satisfy our own emotions. We become focused more on the enjoyment of our own feelings than on worship of the Almighty. The primary reason we must not cling to spiritual highs is that they too often play into our fallen nature. Some of what we assume to be love for the Lord is self-centered, a love that is twisted in on itself.

In order to pursue the Lord and the Lord alone, we must be painfully honest about our motives, even our motivation in prayer and worship. As humbling as it is, we must admit that we often turn to God to get what we want. Such brutal honesty leads to self-knowledge, and sober self-knowledge is the antithesis of our natural inclination toward self-focus. Recognizing our human predisposition to self-absorption, we must face the less-than-flattering motives behind much of what we do. How often we seek only our own comfort and ease in life! Hadewijch concludes:

> We have too much self-will, and we want too much repose, and we seek too much ease and peace. We are too easily tired, and dejected, and disconsolate. We seek too much consolation from God and men. . . . [Thus] we remain not fully grown in the spiritual life.[11]

Therefore, she says, at the appropriate time the Lord withdraws the wonderful feelings so that such spiritual consolations do not feed our addictive nature. God weans us from emotional experience so we can mature. As long as we focus on sweetness, we will be stunted in our spiritual growth and limited in our understanding of God.

The spiritual weaning process is painful and confusing. During this time, says Hadewijch, "life is miserable beyond all that the human heart can bear." It is painful for people undergoing this process because "nothing in their life satisfies them—either their gifts, or their service, or consolations, or all they can accomplish. For interiorly Love draws them so strongly to her, and they feel Love so vast and so incomprehensible."[12]

WELCOMED TO A BIGGER PICTURE OF GOD

The reason we must be weaned—the reason we are not satisfied with spiritual sensation or even Christian service—is that our souls are made for God alone. Emotional pleasures, human praises and popular ministry cannot fill our hearts. Instead, we were meant for full relationship with the Lord. We were created to be contented by God's love and in return to give that love back to him. Nothing less than God in his fullness will truly satisfy our hearts. We dare not settle for delightful feelings; rather, we must relinquish early expressions of love in order to relate with the incomprehensible Trinity. We need to move on to a more complete love that encounters God as God.

Hadewijch emphasizes the inevitable pain of love. Although she employs the courtly language of romance, her concern is something far more noble: our maturation as believers. Emotional dryness is not merely an unavoidable event or unfortunate accident; rather, it is a necessary component in our course of Christian growth.

This stripping process invites us to see a grander picture of God. The Lord is not simply the giver of sweet feelings, nor is our relationship with him confined to moments of spiritual consolation and ecstasy. In order for us to grasp that larger concept of God and enjoy that broader relationship with him, our hearts need to be expanded.

We are created to grow into an adult relationship with the Lord, and we will remain unfulfilled until we come into the fullness of that relationship. Therefore, Hadewijch exhorts her readers to be "content to be deprived of sweet repose for the sake of this great totality of God!"[13]

ASSESSING SPIRITUAL EXPERIENCE TODAY

Hadewijch's counsel is much needed in our day. First, she helps us affirm the spiritual delights we experience. At times we do feel God's reassuring nearness and divine touch profoundly, and it is indeed sweet. Noted author on the deeper spiritual life A. W. Tozer termed this encounter God's "manifest presence."[14] While God is omnipresent—current everywhere all the time—he does not reveal that presence the same way at all times. In his sovereign plan, he chooses to manifest himself in tangible ways at specific times in our lives.

If it is genuine, that divine touch will transform us. A wholesome experience of spiritual sweetness draws us away from worldly pleasures to an intimate relationship with Christ. As we delight in God's presence, the lure of the world loses its grip. The more we have tasted and seen the goodness of the Lord, the less creaturely pleasures exert a pull on us.

The value of affective experience should not be underestimated. Those who never fully taste God the Father's goodness often find it difficult to realize how much he loves them. God's loving-kindness remains a theological proposition in their minds rather than the driving force of their lives. As a result, they are often more susceptible to the fading pleasures of the world and liable to follow Christ in a halfhearted manner. Loving the Lord with our whole being and unabashed emotion is foundational to a full relationship with God.

The fact that such experience eventually fades for most Christians does not mean we should reject our early enjoyment of spiritual sweetness. Throughout her writings Hadewijch emphasizes how much she values the wonderful consolations of her younger years and never apologizes for her personal encounters with the Almighty. Likewise the apostle Paul highlights his experience of Christ on the Damascus road (Acts 9) and his ecstatic transport into God's presence (2 Corinthians 12).

However, while many of us experience wonderful feelings in the early years of our walk with the Almighty, these sensations do not last forever. In time the euphoria and powerful feelings of falling in love dissipate. Like any close friendship, our relationship with God cannot remain in a permanent state of blissful springtime. At some point we must let go of the early blush of emotional love in order to enter into a fuller, more mature relationship with the eternal God.

When we no longer feel God's touch as we have in the past, we often wonder where he has gone. Because we have become accustomed to consolation and the delightfulness of his company, we assume he has abandoned us. Frustrated and confused, we often blame ourselves for somehow chasing him away. When we do not sense his immediate presence, we are thrown into inner torment.

However, we contemporary believers are often afraid to be as blunt about this anguish as Hadewijch and the women of her day were. Because we know God has promised never to leave us or forsake us, we think we are betraying him if we express how abandoned we feel. Thus we pretend that everything is all right and deny that we are in a season of God's apparent absence. As a result, we buffer ourselves from learning the lessons that the Lord has in store for us.

The reality of the Christian life is this: although the Lord never leaves us, at times it feels like he does. While God does not change, our experience of him certainly does. The way we encounter his presence is anything but consistent. We are not alone in this experience, though. A careful reading of the Psalms will disclose how common this sense of separation from the Lord is. "Why, O LORD, do you stand far off? Why do you hide yourself in times of trouble?" cries the psalmist in Psalm 10:1. Rather than denying the experience of abandonment, Psalm 89:46 asks, "How long, O LORD? Will you hide yourself forever?" Perhaps the most agonizing cry of Scripture is that of David in Psalm 22:1—so poignant that Jesus employs it from the cross to express his agony: "My God, my God, why have you forsaken me? Why are you so far from saving me, so far from the words of my groaning?"

Like David and the other psalmists, we also experience a sense of God's absence and question where he has gone. We feel the Lord's love is somehow being taken from us and feel great anguish. This is the greatest distress we encounter in our Christian life. Many of us become numb inside; we stop allowing ourselves

to feel so we do not have to suffer the pain. Some of us try to ignore what we are going through and deny our experience. Still
others of us give up on faith altogether and want to walk away
from the Lord. Rather than ignoring our sense of God's absence or
trying to escape it, we need to express our pain just as David articulates his heart's cry.

OUR ADDICTIVE NATURE

The truth of the Christian journey is that we naturally go through
times of spiritual sweetness and seasons of emotional emptiness.
The danger of the sweet times is that we become attached to them.
In truth, we become addicted to our own feelings. When this happens, we become self-focused and begin to crave an emotional fix,
as it were, every time we meet with God.

When gone to seed, self-focus becomes addiction. The distorted
desires in our lives manifest themselves in addictions that eventually enslave us. We become addicted to food, drink and entertainment. We become dependent on anything that provides us pleasure or dulls our pain. This includes our own emotions, which can
give us the same chemical jolt we gain from drugs or alcohol.[15] We
can even become addicted to spiritual experiences, such as the
"worship high," and find that we crave an emotional trip instead
of actually glorifying the Lord.[16]

Therefore we must break free from our addictions. We must be
weaned if we are to come into a mature relationship with God. We
see this truth reflected in the course of human development.
Young children must be weaned if they are to grow into adoles-
cence and adulthood. If they are not, they develop a very limited—
and very selfish—understanding of their mother. Likewise we
must be liberated from our dependence on spiritual sweetness if
we are to mature as believers.

It is important for us to realize that the waning of elevated
emotions is normal. Although distressing, the decline of sweet

feelings is natural and needs to be embraced. If we are willing to endure such wounding love, we will grow into the fullness of relationship with God we desire. Hadewijch assures us that the coming and going of our feelings is to be expected and that we need not panic. Just as the Lover departs in the Song of Songs, so does our sense of Christ's presence—but it will return. "Do not ask him for spiritual joys in any sort of repose or consolation, unless this is as he himself wills. Let him come and go according to his holy will."[17] Clinging to spiritual sweetness leads only to frustration and discouragement. If we submit our will to the Lord's and allow him to "come and go" at will, we will be at peace in our relationship with him.

Painful as the process may be, according to Hadewijch there is no other path to spiritual maturity. Although it is difficult to release the spiritual consolations to which we have become accustomed, our hearts ultimately long for a deeper understanding of God than simply the one who gives us good feelings. The goal of the Christian life is that we develop in our relationship with the Lord, that we "be built up until we all reach . . . the knowledge of the Son of God and become mature" (Ephesians 4:12-13).

Through the loss of our initial inner consolations, our affections are purified and set free from their reliance on feelings and spiritual sweetness. In this process our hearts become fixed securely on Christ. Such a purging process is unbelievably painful. Those who take the road that leads to maturity find themselves on a challenging path. If we endure the agony, however, our hearts will be cleansed of their false affections. As a result we will truly love the Lord with everything inside of us and pursue intimacy with him as never before.

Personal Response
Drinking from Springs of Living Water

Reflection and Journaling

How do you desire to experience spiritual intimacy with Christ? In what ways have you encountered spiritual sweetness in your relationship with the Lord?

How have you enjoyed wonderful inner connection with God in the past, and how are you currently experiencing spiritual sweetness in your life? In what ways has that inner consolation drawn you away from worldly pleasure and wooed you to Jesus?

If those feelings have faded in your life, how have you responded to that sense of loss? In what ways would you say you have gone numb inside? How can you embrace this time of withdrawal in order to gain a greater picture of God?

Scripture

Read Psalm 16. How have you experienced fullness of joy in God's presence? What are the pleasures you have received from the Almighty's right hand?

Read Psalm 89, especially verses 46-49. In what ways do you identify with David's question: "O Lord, where is your former great love?"

Creativity and Action

What movements express your elation with Jesus' presence—lifting your hands, clapping, shouting or dancing? All of these are employed throughout the Scriptures to convey joy and praise. Take some time to worship the Lord and communicate to him your delight in his love.

If you enjoy artwork, create a piece that depicts your early joy in the Lord and perhaps your later loss of that spiritual springtime. What colors and lines express your early experience of sweetness? How are these contrasted with later developments in your life?

Community

Who is a wise older believer with whom you can share your journey? Find a friend, mentor or spiritual director with whom you can talk about your experience.

How have you felt discouraged by difficult times or the waning of God's sweetness in your life? What passages of Scripture could you memorize? How can Hadewijch's life encourage you in the coming days?

7

Valiant Knights and Untamed Wilderness

Hadewijch Challenges Us to Take the Risk

Therefore I am now going to allure her;
I will lead her into the desert
and speak tenderly to her.

HOSEA 2:14

He who wills to dare the wilderness of Love
Shall understand Love:
Her coming, her going.

HADEWIJCH OF BRABANT

CHIVALRY WAS IN FULL BLOOM in thirteenth-century Europe. Traveling troubadours sang of knights in shining armor who lost life and limb to prove their love for their noble ladies. Poets praised these same ladies for their longing love and suffering souls as they awaited the return of their valiant heroes. The medieval world was ablaze with courtly romance and gallantry.

The central theme of the minstrels' courtly ballads was love— *minne* in medieval German and Dutch. In fact, the bards who wandered the countryside singing the praises of romantic love were called *minnesingers*—those who sing of love. They extolled the virtues of love's deep desire and its unquenchable longing, of love's great suffering and its ultimate reward. Such was the setting of the great spiritual renewal in the high Middle Ages.

Hadewijch was well-versed in the courtly love poetry of the *minnesingers*. Coming from a wealthy family, she had been afforded a good education and knew both Dutch and Latin. She read about knights in love with the noblewomen of the castle and ladies who longed to reunite with their protectors. As she heard these tales of chivalrous romance, she could not help but notice the parallels to her own relationship with Christ. Had she not experienced intimate tryst with the Almighty Protector? Did she not savor the sweetness of his personal presence? Was she not also a lady who longed to see her Lord again and who wondered why he was at times delayed? Thus the Belgian Beguine adapted the genre of her day to depict the dynamics of the Christian life.

Hadewijch detailed her relationship with Jesus in beautiful poetry. Writing sensitive verse with structure, rhythm and rhyme, she described the joys and pains of being in love with the Lord. Hadewijch wrote in Dutch rather than Latin. In fact, she was the first major author of the Dutch language. She left behind a body of literature—poems, letters and visions from the Lord—that is a goldmine of wisdom. Her spiritual insights have been quoted by Christian writers through the centuries, and her poetry is studied in Belgian schools today.

SPIRITUAL KNIGHTS

In her writing Hadewijch employs the same themes as the *minnesingers*. She tells the tale of intimacy with God as a noble romance and explores the experience of spiritual sweetness. Then, in a brilliant literary twist, she changes the gender of her imagery. Hadewijch—like all Christians in this life—must become the strong knight proving his loyalty to Love (*minne*). In courtly poetry the knight risks life and limb to serve his lady and gain her approval. He is often away from her for long periods of time on dangerous quests, and even when he returns, the lady is frequently fickle and pays him little attention.

We are knights, asserts Hadewijch. Our love for the Lord is agonizing because as long as we are in this life we are away on an expedition. We cannot enjoy immediate intimacy with our heavenly Lover. We are spiritual knights in God's service here below and must be ready to prove our love to him, remaining faithful even when we do not experience the emotional rewards of our relationship.

Thus we learn to accept the contingencies of life and fluctuations of love. By suffering the vicissitudes of *minne* we demonstrate our commitment to the Lord. Although love causes us pain, all suffering seems minor in light of Christ's affliction for us. Hadewijch challenges us to endure hardship as brave spiritual knights, learning long-suffering through pain and disappointment. She calls us to be valiant in a love affair far more romantic—and much more real—than that sung of in the ballads of the troubadours. We endure for the eternal prize of love.

HALFHEARTED PURSUIT OF CHRIST
The problem is that too many believers commence the life of faith only to find it much more difficult than they first thought. Like the king who engages in battle and realizes that his forces are much too small (see Luke 14:31-33), these would-be disciples fail to count the cost before they begin.

In her writing Hadewijch describes such Christians. Early in their walk of faith these believers enjoy the taste of God's love but become disillusioned when they discover that it will cost them dearly to be a knight for Christ. They are surprised to learn that spiritual growth entails much hard work.

Instead of unreserved love and commitment to the Lord, these Christians settle for worldly satisfaction and consolation. As a result they never know the fullness of God's affection but forever "remain out of sweet Love's ken." They live the Christian life unenthusiastically and shrink back from the inevitable pain. Out of fear, they cower and do not completely engage in an unconditional relationship with the Lord. They fear that an uncompromising life of faith will demand too much from them. In one of her poems in stanzas Hadewijch writes,

> Ignoble persons of small perception
> Fear the cost will be too high:
> Therefore they withdraw from Love,
> From whom all good would have come to them.[1]

Feeble faith, however, gets them nowhere. When they shrink back from God in an attempt to keep from being hurt, they ultimately build a wall around their hearts. And while that wall protects them from potential pain, it also shields their hearts from being loved. In the end, fear robs them of the great joy of an intimate fellowship with the God of all love.

SPARE NOTHING!

Therefore, throughout her poems Hadewijch exhorts us not to withhold our hearts from Christ, no matter the cost. We must not hesitate or be afraid of pain. "If anyone wishes to content Love," she asserts, "I counsel him to spare himself in nothing."[2] Love costs everything. We will inevitably be wounded along the way, but God is good and will heal those wounds. If we endure until the end, even what seemed to be loss along the way ends up as gain. In poetic verse she states:

> Bitter and dark and desolate
> Are Love's ways in the beginning of love;
> Before anyone is perfect in Love's service,

He often becomes desperate:
Yet where he imagines losing, it is all gain.
 How can one experience this?
By sparing neither much nor little,
 But giving himself totally in love.[3]

Even in the midst of darkness and desolation we must maintain our focus and direct our desire completely toward the Lord and his love. Despite the heartache that we must experience in the process of spiritual maturation, Hadewijch dares us to give ourselves fully to God in love:

He whom Love by all this proves to be noble
Becomes, thanks to the pains of love, so bold
That he proclaims: "Love, I am all yours!
I have nothing but you to revive me.
O noble Love, be all mine!"[4]

The fact that love can be heart-rending is no reason to avoid relationship. Our attempt to shield ourselves from hurt only blocks us from the true joys of intimate fellowship with the Lord. The reason we can ultimately surrender ourselves to the Almighty is his faithfulness. Although the sense of God's absence is agonizing, we ultimately trust in his goodness. Therefore we must persevere and not become disheartened. "Although, too, you sometimes feel such affliction in your heart that it seems to you [that] you are forsaken by God, do not be discouraged by it," exhorts Hadewijch. "For verily I say to you: Whatever misery we endure with good will and for God is pleasing to God in every respect."[5] This exhortation echoes that of Hebrews 12:

"My son, do not make light of the Lord's discipline,
 and do not lose heart when he rebukes you,
because the Lord disciplines those he loves,
 and he punishes everyone he accepts as a son." . . .

No discipline seems pleasant at the time, but painful. Later on, however, it produces a harvest of righteousness and peace for those who have been trained by it. Therefore, strengthen your feeble arms and weak knees. (Hebrews 12:5-12)

JOURNEY INTO THE WILDERNESS

Using further imagery, Hadewijch bids us venture into the desert wilds of the spiritual life as we progress in the Lord. When inner sweetness runs dry and we wonder where the Lord has gone, we enter a dark and deserted place. Some three centuries after Hadewijch, John of the Cross used the phrase "dark night" to describe the anguish of the soul, the confusion and gloom we experience during God's purging process in our lives. Hadewijch's writing and that of others in the thirteenth and fourteenth centuries were forerunners of John's theme.

Scripture is replete with accounts of men and women who traverse the wilderness. The Sinai Peninsula and Judean wilderness are both desert territories, dry and dangerous lands in which to journey. Travel through such wasteland requires perseverance. On our spiritual pilgrimage, the desert is a place that tests our resolve: it sorts out those who are only halfhearted in their faith.

The wilderness works on us. It strips away all that is unnecessary. It purges us of our demand to be pampered. Ultimately, the wilderness prepares us to meet God in a whole new way. The desert is difficult, but it is also a place to encounter God.

Those who survive the desert often meet God there face to face, as Scripture attests. On the verge of death, Hagar encounters God in the desert of Beersheba and receives a promise of the Almighty's protection and blessing (Genesis 21:8-20). In the desert of Sinai, Moses hears Yahweh in the burning bush and also meets him there during the exodus to receive the Ten Commandments (Exodus 3; 19). Elijah travels forty days and nights through the wilderness to the same mountain where the Lord speaks to him in a still, small voice (1 Kings 19:12-13). The word of the Lord comes to John the Baptist in the desert (Luke 3:2). Jesus fasts forty days in the wilderness where he is tested (Luke 4:1-13), and Paul spends three years in the wilderness after his conversion (Galatians 1:18).

Wilderness imagery likewise pervades the pages of the thirteenth-century women writers. Hosea 2:14 is one of their theme verses. It weaves together their self-understanding as God's beloved bride and their encounter with the Divine in the wilderness: "Therefore I am now going to allure her; I will lead her into the desert and speak tenderly to her."

For Hadewijch, those times when she cannot sense God's love constitute the darkest wilderness in life. In a literal desert we long for water but are not satisfied; in the desert of love, we yearn for feelings of God's presence but our desires go unmet. For Hadewijch, love turns to a dry desert when the initial sweetness of relationship diminishes and the season of endurance begins. We come into the Lord's highest place of spiritual growth and intimacy only if we persevere to the end. In her poem "Daring the Wilderness," Hadewijch prays for those who are willing to brave the desert:

> Now may God help those
> Who would gladly do all things
> According to Love's wishes,
> And who will gladly traverse the deep wilderness
> To the land of love,
> Where they are often placed in afflictions
> And are subject to Love in all things
> In heavy chains:
> Thus love holds them heavy laden
> In the continual fire
> Of Love.
>
> Here is Love's guarantee:

When Love with love finds fidelity in anyone
Who for love's sake undergoes all pains,
　　Sweet and harmless,
Full satisfactions shall be known to him
　　　　　In love.[6]

The valiant Beguine calls us to spare nothing in our pursuit of
the Lord. She challenges us not to back away but to take the adventure:

O soul, creature
And noble image,
Risk the adventure![7]

DARE THE ADVENTURE!

Recognizing the pain that substantive spiritual growth entails,
Hadewijch instructs the young Beguines around her to hazard
the adventure of spiritual progress—the gamble of wholeheartedly falling in love with Jesus. She summons them to open their
whole being up to a love relationship with the Lord, knowing
they will encounter both bliss and heartache. The two always go
together in love.

Although Hadewijch knows that love hurts, she maintains that
the only way to follow God is unconditionally, and she welcomes
us into an adventurous relationship with the Almighty that will
engage all our strength and energy. We cannot enter into loving
union with the Lord halfheartedly. From the beginning to the end
of Scripture, God invites us into a total consecration of our lives to
him—an unreserved relationship that entails our entire being. In
another of her poems in stanzas, Hadewijch exhorts us not to fear
the pain or expense of pursuing Christ:

He who wishes thus to progress in love
Must not fear expense, or harm,
Or pain; but faithfully confront

The strictest commands of Love,
And be submissive with faultless service
In all her comings and in all her goings:
Anyone who behaved thus, relying on Love's fidelity,
Would stand to the end, having become all love in Love.[8]

CONQUERING AND BEING CONQUERED

We must be bold in love, says Hadewijch. Although God does not need us, he delights in our search for him. Just as lovers want their loved one to pursue them, so the Lord revels in our wholehearted pursuit of him. Hadewijch challenges us to address Love:

I greet you, Love, with undivided love,
And I am brave and daring;
I will yet conquer your power,
Or I will lose myself in the attempt![9]

How is it that we can conquer love? We do so with longing desire. We must wrestle with love until we prevail. Just as Jacob wrestled with the Lord in Genesis 32:22-32, we must summon the courage to engage with God. When he sees that we desire him above all earthly possessions, other people and even spiritual blessings, he allows us to "conquer" him.

And if anyone then dares to fight Love with longing,
Wholly without heart and without mind,
And love counters this longing with her longing:
That is the force by which we conquer Love.

Thenceforward, whether with joy or pain,
If anyone can dare to fight Love with ardor,
Love cannot resist the violence of the assault:
But he shall abide firm in the storm, conformed to Love.[10]

Jacob wrestles and wins. Yet ultimately it is God who conquers. From the day of that hand-to-hand encounter with Yahweh, Jacob is a broken man who limps as a reminder of God's omnipotence. In the same manner, if we are faithful to Love through the ups and downs of our relationship with the Lord, he will conquer us. "Jacob is everyone who conquers; by the power of Love, he conquered God, in order to be conquered himself," writes Hadewijch. "Whoever wishes to wrestle with God must set himself to conquer in order to be conquered."[11]

WILDERNESS TRANSFORMATION

Wrestling with God in the wilderness transforms us. Hadewijch bids us as her readers to alloww God to have his way in our lives so that in every attitude and action we might be "conformed to the likeness of his Son" (Romans 8:29). When God's love conquers us it changes us from deep within.

Change is never easy; it always comes at a price. True transformation is agonizing. It is slow and painful, requiring tremendous perseverance on our part. Because it is an excruciating process, most of us avoid it as long as we possibly can—until it is more painful to stay where we are than it is to change, as the saying goes. Hadewijch knows how difficult it is, yet she prays for such transformation. Above all she desires that we be conformed to the image of Christ, as she writes in her poem "The Need of All Needs":

> O sublime nature, true Love,
> When will you make my nature so fair
> That it will be wholly conformed to your nature?
> For I wish to be wholly conformed.
> If all that is other in me were yours,
> Everything that is yours would be altogether mine:
> I should burn to ashes in your fire![12]

The Lord's desire is to renovate us from the inside out, making substantive alterations at the root level of our beings. Our old nature must be crucified daily, or "burned to ashes," as Hadewijch phrases it, in order for our new nature to be manifested. Such transformation means that we must encounter God who is "a consuming fire" (Hebrews 12:29). Only his burning holiness can truly transform us.

When God changes us he makes us into his image. That divine likeness is love itself. If we are faithful to the Lord through the hard times as well as the good, he will conform us into Christ's character and fashion us into love. Spiritual formation includes bitter cold spells as well as wonderful, warm summertime. It is during the fallow time of winter that God often does his deepest work in our character—stripping our dependence on feelings, cleansing our desires and testing the resolve of our heart. In her poem "Laying Siege to Love," Hadewijch writes:

> Spring comes in new; and the old winter season,
> After its long reign, vanishes.
> Were anyone ready in Love's service,
> He would receive from her a reward:
> New consolation and new power;
> And if he loved Love with the power of love,
> He would speedily become love with Love.[13]

If we endure through the long winter season in our spiritual life, we will be changed. If we persevere, we will indeed come to springtime. There we receive fresh consolations and find that we are being transformed into love.

LOVE WILL REWARD IN FULL

Although we do not understand the ways of the Lord, the Lord is always faithful. If we do not abandon our love relationship with him—if we are willing to endure the hard times as well as the sweet—we will be rewarded in full. Hadewijch repeatedly promises us that although Love comes late, she always compensates us for our faithfulness:

Love always rewards, even though she comes late.
Those who forsake themselves for her,
And follow her highest counsel,
And remain steadfast in longing,
  She shall compensate with love.[14]

As we persevere through the depths of the dark times, we come
to a new confidence that God is indeed for us and with us. Despite
our circumstances, our senses or our feelings, we come to the realization that God is perhaps most present in the midst of our
pain. Going through the process seems to take an eternity, but in
compensating us "the Lord is not slow in keeping his promise, as
some understand slowness" (2 Peter 3:9).

If we abandon ourselves to love, we will not be disappointed in
the long run. The Lord is faithful; he does not overlook our service
to him and our love for him. "God is not unjust," asserts Hebrews
6:10; "he will not forget your work and the love you have shown."
Although at times along the way it seems that the Lord has over-
looked us, he always repays us:

In love no action is lost
That was ever performed for Love's sake;
Love always repays, late or soon;
Love is always the reward of love.[15]

In particular Love rewards us with love. God repays us by
bringing us into intimate union with himself. Our hearts' deepest
desire is not for recognition or even spiritual experience. Rather it
is for a full realization of God's love for us. Here we forget about
ourselves and become conscious of nothing other than being loved
by God. What a wonderful thing it is when we simply forget about
ourselves and are not even aware of how we are "experiencing"
God's presence. Instead we are completely focused on the Divine
and are cognizant of nothing but him!

What seems to the loved soul the most beautiful encounter
Is that it should love the Beloved so fully
And so gain knowledge of the Beloved with love
That nothing else be known by it
Except: "I am love conquered by Love!"[16]

WILDERNESS TODAY

The deeper life to which we are called is a transformed existence. Once we are forgiven of sin, we are not meant to loiter at the starting line of the race of faith. To the contrary, we are summoned to run toward the goal of maturity. In our day as in Hadewijch's, many Christians attempt to lead a safe, comfortable walk with God. Such meager faith, however, leads to a life of tedium and weariness. Many believers become bored in their walk with Christ because they fail to truly follow him. They try to "play it safe" and refrain from abandoning themselves unreservedly to the Lord. As a result these fainthearted Christians live a lackluster life.

Being a true disciple of Jesus, however, is never dull. In the gospels the twelve are often frightened, confused and frustrated—but never bored. If believers are weary of their Christian walk, it is because they have failed to follow Christ on the adventure on which he desires to take them.

Such a commitment can cost us much, as Hebrews 11 demonstrates. While many men and women in this biblical "hall of fame" receive miraculous deliverance as they trust in the Lord, others suffer greatly and some experience martyrdom. Yet all of them are praised as great exemplars of faith. In light of their example, we are exhorted to run with endurance the race set before us and not to shy away from the challenge. "We are not of those who shrink back and are destroyed," contends Hebrews 10:39, "but of those who believe and are saved."

Genuine pilgrimage is a valiant expedition. This adventure

ushers us from the land of dissimilitude—where we are unlike Christ, where our thoughts, words and deeds are inexorably tainted by fallen human nature—to the place where our minds are filled with our Redeemer's thoughts and all we do is directed by his indwelling presence. The areas where we most need to change are those where we are least like our Lord. In his *Invitation to a Journey*, Robert Mulholland states, "The process of being conformed to the image of Christ takes place primarily at the points of our unlikeness to Christ's image. . . . This can be uncomfortable. We would much rather have our spiritual formation focus on those places where we are pretty well along the way."[17]

Transformation takes time, however. Genuine Christianity requires long-term growth. The process of sanctification is a lifelong progression by which we daily put off our old self in order to put on a new existence in Christ. To have "Christ formed" in us (Galatians 4:19), our whole view of reality needs to be renovated. We must "not conform any longer to the pattern of this world, but be transformed by the renewing of [our] mind" (Romans 12:2). If we persevere in that process, we will be changed to be ever more like our Lord. The apostle Paul promises in 2 Corinthians 3:18 that "we all, who with unveiled faces contemplate the Lord's glory, are being transformed into his likeness with ever-increasing glory, which comes from the Lord, who is the Spirit" (TNIV).

FORSAKING OUR FALSE SELF

So why must we encounter the wilderness? More than anything else, the wilderness purges us of our false self. The false self that within us that tries to provide for our own self-interest, assuming that God is not actively working for us. Called the "imposter" by Brennan Manning in his book *Abba's Child*, the false self tries to make us look good and prop up our wounded self-perception. It is the "glittering image" we want to portray to others so they do not see the broken and less-than-glamorous reality of who we actually are.[18]

Because our false self is ultimately our fallen nature attempting its own salvation, Robert Mulholland poignantly describes it as a fearful self, a protective self and a possessive self in his book *The Deeper Journey*. Those attempts to save ourselves turn sour, and that sinful nature begins to manifest itself as the manipulative, self-promoting, indulgent and distinction-making self that compares itself to others and tries to present itself as better.[19]

Our false self even pervades our spiritual life. Unwittingly we approach our growth in the Lord with the same flaws that affect our approach to life and relationships. Fearful of not looking good in Christian circles, we put up a pious front and vigorously protect our image. Mulholland aptly describes this as our "religious false self," which is "rigorous in religiosity, devoted in discipleship and sacrificial in service—without being in loving union with God."[20]

All of this self-focus is desire gone awry. Instead of pursuing the Lord and reaching out to others in love, we turn our attention on our own activities, gifts and spiritual self-image. In the end, we are trying to manage God. "The 'God' within our box . . . becomes a construct, an idol, that enables us to maintain control of what we call 'God' as well as continue to be in control of our existence. To put it succinctly, whenever we attempt to have God in our life on our terms, we are a religious false self."[21]

Because our false self is so entwined with our development, our relationships, our approach to life and our very personality, radical surgery is required to remove it from us. That surgery is the wilderness. Although Hadewijch and John of the Cross do not use the terminology of "false self," they describe the same fallen, human condition and recognize that we cannot set ourselves free from it no matter how many spiritual disciplines we might practice. Rather it must be burned out of hearts through the painful—but effective—process of entering the wilderness.

That wilderness may look different from one person to the next because we have differing false selves. "We are led into the deserts of our hearts to be redeemed, liberated from our seductive but addictive desires, to become recommitted to God at a deeper level of surrender in love," observes James Houston in *The Desire: Satisfying the Heart*. "There is not just one kind of desert experience, but as many as there are differing personalities and personal stories, yours and mine."[22] For Hadewijch, the desert involved giving up intimate feelings of the Lord's closeness. For us, it may be something very different. However, we must all face the cleansing wilderness.

"For the 'perfectionist,'" continues Houston, "there is the desert of imperfection. . . . The 'idealist' . . . is placed in the desert of ordinariness. . . . The 'controller' ends up in the desert of weakness, and is made vulnerable to the threat of the chaotic in a wholly new way."[23] God sets each of us in a custom-made wilderness so that we can face, and be purged of, that false self that has tried to control the world around us and make things go our way.

ANSWERING THE CALL

Much contemporary Christian teaching focuses on triumph and neglects the painful path to real transformation. It ignores the insidious, all-pervasive undercurrent of our fallen self and settles for a quick fix accompanied by a superficial claim to victory. The call to take the adventure is crucial in light of our instant-gratification culture. The path is bound to take us through the wilderness where we are purged and where we meet God face to face.

Hadewijch invites us to hold nothing back as we follow Christ. As spiritual knights we will face the perilous wilderness, but she assures us that the venture will be worth it all. Although it seems that the Lord comes late, he always comes—transforming us by his burning presence and filling us with his eternal love.

Personal Response
Drinking from Springs of Living Water

Reflection and Journaling

In your journal describe how your pursuit of Christ has been more painful than you first anticipated. Do you tend to be timid or valiant like a knight when challenges face you? How can you take courage from Hadewijch's challenge and cultivate a knight's attitude in your life?

In what ways can you identify with the wilderness imagery of Scripture? How has your spiritual pilgrimage taken you into a long, dry place? How do you need to persevere?

If you are currently in a "dark night of the soul," describe it in your journal. How do you believe the Lord wants you to embrace the situation where you are right now?

Scripture

Study Psalm 10 and Psalm 13. In a journal, write how you identify with the psalmist, as well as Hadewijch, in your longing for the Lord's presence and your questioning why he seems absent.

Read one of the biblical desert accounts mentioned in the chapter. Which of these women or men do you identify with and why? What can you learn from their wilderness experience?

Read Hebrews 10:35–12:13. How can you follow the example of the men and women of faith described here? In what ways do you need to persevere and not shrink back?

Creativity and Action

What imagery in this chapter captured your imagination: ladies of the castle, knighthood, the wilderness, the false self? Try your hand at putting some of your reflections down in poetic form. It does not need to be perfect—just real.

If you are musically inclined, take some of those thoughts and set them to music. A melody often expresses our inner stirrings as much as words. Perhaps you will never perform your song for anyone but God. If you have courage like Hadewijch, however, try sharing your poetry or song with others. You never know how it will touch someone else. Hadewijch likely never dreamed that her works would experience such revival after eight hundred years!

Community

Write a brief description of a long, dry time in your life—either that you are experiencing now or that you have gone through in the past. Then describe ways God might have made himself known in the wilderness or how you met him in a new way in the desert. With a trusted friend or in your small group, share your story and have others share theirs. Take time to pray for each one.

8

Flowing In and Out of God's Presence

Mechthild of Magdeburg Offers a Balance of Solitude and Service

Jesus replied, "'Love the Lord your God with all your heart and with all your soul and with all your mind.' This is the first and greatest commandment. And the second is like it: 'Love your neighbor as yourself.'"

MATTHEW 22:37-39

[God]
When I shine, you shall glow.
When I flow, you shall become wet.
When you sigh, you draw my divine heart into you. . . .

[Soul]
Lord, then I shall persevere in hunger and thirst
In pursuing and in pleasure
Till that playful hour
When from your divine mouth
The chosen words shall flow
That are heard by no one
But the soul alone
That has stripped itself of the earth
And puts her ear next to your mouth.
She, indeed, grasps the treasure of love!

MECHTHILD OF MAGDEBURG

MECHTHILD GREW UP NEAR MAGDEBURG, GERMANY, some ninety miles southwest of Berlin. A contemporary of Hadewijch, she was born in 1207 or 1208. From a very young age she thirsted for God. First experiencing a powerful divine touch when she was twelve years old, she found the Lord's sweet presence so wonderful that it "spoiled for me all worldly sweetness," as she wrote later. After this experience she pursued Christ with little interest in what the world had to offer. God "let me experience such delightful sweetness, such holy knowledge, and such incomprehensible wonders that I found little enjoyment in earthly things."[1]

Desiring to progress in her relationship with Jesus, Mechthild moved to Magdeburg, where she joined a group of Beguines in 1230. She was twenty-three years old when she arrived, and she spent the next forty years in that city. While we know few details of her life, it seems that she was promoted to be the mistress of a Beguine community where she helped younger women to grow in the Lord.

Like Hadewijch, Mechthild employed the courtly love poetry of her day. Freely adapting the genre's style, themes and vocabulary to help her express her inner longings for Jesus, Mechthild was innovative in the use of her native German language as she penned prose, poetry and at times a hybrid of the two.[2] Because she was not trained in Latin, however, she never considered herself to be truly educated.

During her years in Magdeburg, Mechthild began to compose her work on the spiritual life, *Flowing Light of the Godhead*, consisting of seven books. She wrote *Flowing Light* not simply for the spiritual elite but to provide encouragement and direction for all believers who yearn to grow in their relationship with God. The initial impetus for this volume probably came from her confessor, Heinrich of Halle, who heard Mechthild describe the joys and struggles of her inner pilgrimage and recognized the wisdom she had to offer. A Dominican friar who served as spiritual director for many Beguines, Heinrich appreciated Mechthild's passion for the Lord and the depth of her experience. He helped to edit the first five books of her work.

Flowing Light of the Godhead

Mechthild's *Flowing Light* explores the progression of the Christian life as it describes some of her own experience and growth. She depicts spiritual formation not in terms of practicing disciplines, but rather as a love relationship with the triune God. Passion and intimacy pervade Mechthild's writing and her personal experience.

Yet Mechthild's writings maintain a remarkable balance between descriptions of her relationship with the Lord and her connection with others. In the midst of enjoying Jesus' loving presence, she does not neglect to focus on service to others. She situates both vertical and horizontal love in a well-developed trinitarian theology.

Mechthild uses the imagery of the tide streaming out and surging back to describe our rhythm of active ministry and intimate solitude. We pour out in our service to others, then we return to our time alone with the Lord. Mechthild presents a thoughtful harmony between these two impulses of the faith and sees them flowing back and forth, two parts of one whole. Both dynamics are essential to the Christian life, and both are a reflection of God's own flowing forth and surging back—hence the title of her book: *Flowing Light of the Godhead.*[3]

GOD'S LOVE SPLASHES FORTH

Because God is love, he is always giving and ever flowing forth. In beautiful trinitarian language, Mechthild describes the goodness that streams from God. Following a long theological tradition tracing back to Augustine of Hippo, Mechthild depicts God the

Father issuing forth in eternity by speaking the Word, his Son, the second person of the Trinity. The Father and Son then together pour out their love through the Holy Spirit.

The Godhead's radiating love does not stop there. It continues to spill forth in the creation of the world. God flows forth, "sustaining all things by his powerful word" (Hebrews 1:3). Such love splashes out joyfully as God fashions humanity in his own image. Here God overflows in jubilant celebration, says Mechthild: "When God could no longer contain himself, he created the soul and, in his immense love, gave himself to her as her own."[4]

God's love streams into us, filling our hearts with his presence and producing a playful delight in our souls. We respond by pouring our love back to God. In this giving and receiving, love flows back and forth as the tide of personal relationship with the Divine. Thus, Mechthild declares:

> This is the playful flood of love
> That flows mysteriously from God into the soul
> And through his power flows back again according to
>   [the soul's] ability.
> What bliss there is then between them![5]

GOD FLOWS INTO US

Such understanding of God's flowing forth has implications for our lives. We are not called simply to be saved; we are invited into a living, breathing immediacy with the Creator of the universe. The divine flow fills us and draws us into an intimate relationship with the Lord. God floods our hearts with his love and acceptance. We respond by immersing ourselves in this divine tide.

Such flowing love is the wellspring of Mechthild's life. As one who is truly in love, she cannot bear the idea of being parted from her God. She feels she would die if her immediacy with the Lord were ever taken away.

O you pouring God in your gift!
O you flowing God in your love!
O you burning God in your desire!
O you melting God in the union with your beloved!
O you resting God on my breasts!
Without you I cannot exist.[6]

Despite her rapture, Mechthild brings her theology down to a practical plane. She suggests we set aside one full hour each day for the Lord to fill us with that love. Jesus desires such interaction with us: it is to that end that he came to earth, suffered and died for us. Indeed, he loved us so much that he set aside his life with the Father for thirty years to live a humbling, painful existence with us on earth. How then, asks Mechthild, can we be so ungrateful and indifferent as to refuse one hour of our day to give him our undivided attention?

You should readily offer our dear Lord God a free hour, day or night, during which you can pray lovingly and undisturbed. . . . [Christ was willing to] renounce for more than thirty years everything that he found pleasant [so that] he might kiss [you] again and again and embrace [you] with his bare arms. If you were to think about this, how could you act so crudely as not to give him an hour a day in return for those thirty years?[7]

WE FLOW OUT TO OTHERS

After we have been filled in the Lord's presence, we overflow with God's goodness and shower his grace on the world around us. Our experience of God's presence and our ministry to others are integrally linked: we need such solitude with the Lord if we are to have anything to share with others. As we have received, we give God's love to believers and unbelievers alike in our lives.

Thus the Father's divine affection continues to pour out to all humanity. God's love streams to us during our sweet times with him and then it pours forth through us to the world. "The great outflow of divine love that never ceases flows on and on unceasingly and effortlessly in such a sweet course unfailingly that our tiny vessel becomes full and brims over. If we do not block it with self-will, our small vessel is always overflowing with God's favor," writes Mechthild. "Lord, you are full and you fill us as well with your favor. You are great and we are small. How are we to become like you? Lord, you have given us much and we should pass it on in turn."[8]

Our reaching out to others is not simply an act of well-intentioned ministry, but rather it is a continuation of God's own flowing forth. We must be transformed into channels through which God can pour his love and grace, and we truly minister to others when we become conduits of the Lord's compassion. As we serve others, we are instruments of the Holy Spirit, who is God's love poured out to the whole world. Indeed, it is the Father performing acts of kindness through us as we reach out to those around us.

Ministry to others does not proceed from our own will. Indeed, any virtue in our lives comes from the Lord's flowing light shining through us. In poetic verse Mechthild asserts:

I no longer have any virtue;
He serves me with his virtues.
That I ever could do anything good separated from my Lord:
That would be more difficult for me than death.
I dare not, alas, claim credit
For everything that I say about love.
It is God, rather, who is thereby reaching out
To all those chosen in his heart.[9]

We are but channels of God's virtue. Our one need is to be filled with divine power and presence that we can then pass on to others. Each time we pour out, we allow God to fill us afresh so that we never run dry. "Though we are a small vessel, still you have made it full. . . . We are, alas, so tiny that a single little word from God or from Holy Scripture fills us so completely that for the moment we can take in no more. Then we pour the gift back again into the large container that is God. How are we to do this? In holy longing we should pour it over sinners that they be cleansed. If it again becomes full, we should then pour it over [other Christians] that they fight on and become perfect and remain so."[10]

Mechthild models for us a life of faith founded on God's grace. This is the exchanged life. Each day we give God our brokenness and sin. In return, he gives us his love and flows through us to others.

> Daily I offer you whatever I have:
> Nothing but baseness.
> And you, Lord, shall infuse me with your grace.
> Then I can flow from your love.[11]

FLOWING IN PRACTICAL MINISTRY AND HUMBLE LEADERSHIP

Always down to earth, Mechthild offers a variety of concrete ways we can serve others. First, we can pour forth in prayer. Throughout her book Mechthild describes the role of interceding for others. We ought especially to intercede for sinners who are lost without Christ. In addition, we should pray for fellow believers, particularly those who are caught up in a worldly way of life. They need our prayer because they have lost their "noble way of life and [their] sweet intimacy with God. . . . They revile the interior life . . . [and] appear wise outwardly but unfortunately are all fools inwardly."[12]

Likewise we pour out to others when we serve them in practical ways. Mechthild challenges us to actively seek how we can serve the needy and infirm. We should "search out and inquire where the lonely, sick, and prisoners are; and that one soothe them with words and bid them tell you their secret distress, so that you might be able to come to their aid. Woe to those who pass by those who are sick and alone without groans, tears, or any sign of compassion."[13]

James, our Lord's brother, highlights the necessity of such sensible service. "What good is it, my brothers, if a man claims to have faith but has no deeds?" (James 2:14). Then he replies, "Show me your faith without deeds, and I will show you my faith by what I do" (James 2:18). Mechthild likewise confronts us with the rhetorical questions, "What good are lofty words without works of mercy? What good is love of God when joined to rage against good human beings?"[14]

Humble service is especially important for leaders. Mechthild has much to say on the topic of servant leadership. Highly critical of abbots, bishops and popes who wield power and exercise authority to their own advantage, this unassuming Beguine calls for church leaders to return to Jesus' injunctions to his disciples. "If anyone wants to be first," states our Lord, "he must be the very last, and the servant of all" (Mark 9:35). Therefore, Mechthild instructs the priors and prioresses of the monastic houses to wait on those under their care:

> Thus shall you encourage all your brothers as they go forth. You should also raise their spirits when they return. You should go in advance to the guest quarters and with God's liberality make all arrangements for the basic comfort of God's disciples as far as is in your power. Indeed, dear fellow, you should even wash their feet yourself.[15]

If this were not enough, Mechthild admonishes those in leadership to visit the ill to cheer them up as well as perform the most demeaning tasks. "You should visit the infirmary every day and comfort the sick with the consoling words of God and refresh them generously with earthly things, for God is rich beyond all accounting. You should clean for the sick and in God cheerfully laugh with them. You should yourself carry away their personal waste. . . . Then God's sweetness shall flow into you in marvelous ways."[16] Here we see how loving service of others is tied to intimacy with the Lord. When we flow out to others in humility—even emptying their bedpans—God flows afresh into us in marvelous ways.

Our service to others is ultimately God's flowing through us; our works are but the persons of the Godhead pouring through the vessels of our lives. We dare not take credit for any ministry. Everything comes *from* God, manifests *through* him and returns *to* his greater glory:

> For from him and through him to him are all things.
> To him be the glory forever! Amen. (Romans 11:36)

When we remind ourselves of this reality we guard our hearts from pervading pride. "We receive these good works from God's holy humanity [Christ] and perform them through the power of the Holy Spirit. Thus do our works and our life return to the Holy Trinity."[17]

WE FLOW BACK IN INTIMATE RELATIONSHIP

After we have poured out to others, we must flow back into solitude with God. Our coursing out in service and streaming back to God in intimate relationship mirror the motion of the Godhead. Mechthild maintains a marvelous balance of outward ministry and inward intimacy:

> To the degree that we perform good works here, God's holy
>   toil shall light up and shine into our holy toil.
> To the degree that we possess inwardness here in intimacy
>   with God, God's holy intimacy shall richly light up
>   and send sparks into our holy inwardness.[18]

We flow out and back because we are created in the *imago Dei*—

God's image. As Augustine describes, the three persons of the Trinity pour forth in their differentiation of persons and distinction of activity, then surge back to each other in unity and love. In like manner we are created to flow back in intimacy with God when we return to our place of prayer and savor our love relationship with him. In fact, our relationship with the Lord is a participation in the very relationship that the three persons of the Trinity share with each other.

When we have surged back into God's intimate embrace and soak in the Almighty's presence, it is not time to concern ourselves with activity or ministry, no matter how valuable that may be. Service to the Lord cannot replace relationship with him. If we neglect the priority of undivided attention to the Lord, we obstruct God's flowing into us and cut ourselves off from the life-giving source. We hinder the Divine from filling us with his power and presence. "Man can easily block up his heart with an idle thought," observes Mechthild, "so that the restless Godhead that continually toils without toil cannot flow into his soul."[19]

When we become so engrossed in ministry that we fail to set apart sufficient time alone with God, we impede the divine stream of love. Mechthild notes that too often Christians—especially those who are intellectually bright—obstruct the Lord's intimacy. When God begins to touch them with his loving presence, they busy themselves with ministry under the guise that they can be more useful in "external matters" than spending time in intimate prayer with the Lord. Such Christians fend off divine inwardness in the following way:

> When God sees fit to let his divine heart shine forth in love toward the very blessed soul so intensely that a small spark alights on the cold soul and she receives so much that the heart of this person begins to glow, his soul to melt, and his eyes to flow, then our Lord would like to make an earthly

person so heavenly that one actually wants to follow, love, and see God in him. [But] the person's senses say: "No, I can be of much [more] use in external matters."[20]

If we do not take time to draw apart with God, we have nothing to pour forth to others. Rather than busying ourselves with so much activity that we keep the Lord at arm's length, we must allow him to stream afresh into us. We need to wade into the divine flow of intimate solitude and selfless service. In order to maintain such a rhythm we must be careful not to assume more responsibilities than the Lord has allotted us.

ACTIVISM OF TODAY'S CHRISTIAN

Ours is a culture of activity and achievement. How often we expend ourselves all day in evangelism, service and ministry, without pulling back to God's quiet presence, and quickly become exhausted and fragmented. In the midst of our frenetic activism we become disjointed and lose our vital connection with the Lord. As a result, much of our busyness is scattered. We spin in circles. We waste time on entertainment. We claim little of lasting value. While we maintain that we do not have one hour a day to spend with the Lord, we really prefer our hectic, contemporary lifestyle to a deep, personal time with the Savior.

Much of our focus on busyness and activity comes from our cultural assumption that personal identity comes from what we do. James Houston observes that the church today "is full of people who . . . secularize the Christian message by infecting it with a spirit of busyness. They end up defining themselves and their faith by their activities. . . . Unfortunately, despite all the effort, the achiever will always fail at prayer. His competitive spirit makes true prayer impossible."[21]

Although we say we believe in prayer, our actions speak louder than our words. If we are honest, we realize that ultimately we view prayer as impractical. Our overly active lives declare to God and the world that we believe prayer is inefficient. Underneath we are convinced that everything depends on our own effort. We "get trapped in crowded schedules," notes spiritual director Margaret Guenther, "and fall into the dangerous and sinful delusion that we, the administrative assistants of a well-meaning but inefficient CEO God, are really the ones who hold up the world."[22]

To deepen our life in prayer we must stop pretending to be God's efficient administrative assistants and allow our spiritual eyes to be opened to God's activity all around us. Whether we pray or act, God is always prior. As we pursue God we find that he has first been seeking us; however, we will never see his hand at work unless we pull apart to a lonely place, as Jesus does throughout his earthly ministry.

The Beguine from Magdeburg presents a balanced and practical paradigm of spiritual formation and ministry. She portrays a life of rhythm that flows into God's presence and surges out into a needy world, only to return at regular intervals to that life-giving intimacy with the Lord. Her book is instructive to contemporary believers—especially those engaged in ministry. In a world that is shattered, we need to bring healing and wholeness, not further fragmentation. Only as we flow back to God in intimate time with him each day will we experience the wholeness and integrity we hope to share with a broken and hurting world.

LIFE-GIVING SOLITUDE

Solitude is foundational to ministry. Without solitude we are mired in disordered priorities and a twisted perspective on life. "Solitude is one of the deepest disciplines of the spiritual life because it crucifies our need for importance and prominence," insists Richard Foster in his *Devotional Classics*. "Everyone— including ourselves at first—will see our solitude as a waste of good time. We are removed from 'where the action is.' That, of course, is exactly what we need. In silence and solitude God slowly but surely frees us from our egomania."[23]

What happens when you begin to pull back and make room for solitude in your life? In his book *Nurturing Silence in a Noisy Heart*, Wayne Oates answers, "You will experience unasked-for loneliness, which becomes a prelude to the privacy and solitude that you need for the kind of silence that will heal your noisy heart. That silence will enable you to think new thoughts. You will develop green growing edges to a new being you vaguely sense you are becoming as you break out of your old routine."[24]

Service and solitude belong together like the ebb and flow of ocean waves. "A practicing Christian must above all be one who practices the perpetual return of the soul into the inner sanctuary," affirms Thomas Kelly in his classic *A Testament of Devotion*. "There is a way of ordering our mental life on more than one level at once. On one level we may be thinking, discussing, seeing, calculating, meeting all the demands of external affairs. But deep within, behind the scenes, at a profounder level, we may also be in prayer and adoration, song and worship and a gentle receptiveness to divine breathings."[25]

Only when we maintain that inner intimacy with God can we gain divine perspective on all our disparate activities and contending demands. Here we see things from God's vantage point, bringing order to all our misplaced priorities. Kelly continues: "Facts remain facts, when brought into the Presence in the deeper level, but their value, their significance, is wholly realigned. Much apparent wheat becomes utter chaff, and some chaff becomes wheat."[26]

BRINGING IT HOME

How long may I spend alone in God's presence this morning? I love the sweet fellowship with the Lord and could remain the whole day in solitude with him. Yet I know I have responsibilities to fulfill and peo-

ple to serve. What portion of my time needs to flow out to others in the world around me?

Thoughts similar to these run through many of our minds as we seek to maintain a sense of biblical balance in our lives. We are called into an intimate love affair with the Lord, filled with intense desire and deep fulfillment. Yet we cannot remain forever in the prayer "closet," as Jesus calls it in Matthew 6:6 (KJV). We have responsibilities to fulfill and people to serve. Relationship is both vertical and horizontal. Indeed, our love for the Lord, whom we cannot see, is fictitious if it is not fleshed out in our interaction with the people around us.

Jesus asserts that the greatest commandment is to love the Lord with all our heart, soul, mind and strength, and the second is to love our neighbor as ourselves. These two commandments complement each other and entwine one another. Their outworking affects our lives greatly, integrating our intimacy with the Lord and our ministry to others. Often these two dynamics of the Christian life pull us in opposite directions: one toward the solitude of prayer and contemplation, the other toward active service among needy people. Such a balance is difficult to maintain. Most of us swing to one side of the pendulum or the other. Either we focus on "Jesus and me" to the neglect of others, or our personal time with Christ suffers as we busy ourselves with evangelism, service and missions.

The Beguines knew this same tension and sought to hold together both sides. While they pursued an intense personal relationship with God, they never divorced their private devotional life from their acts of kindness toward others. In the Beguine communities they sought to establish a dynamic equilibrium between these two poles of the spiritual life.

No one illustrates that equilibrium more clearly or more memorably than Mechthild. She reminds us that we need both, and she shows us that the key to maintaining this steady rhythm of flowing out to others and pulling back in solitude is the experience of God's presence. If we are truly touched by God's transforming presence during our time alone with him, we will know how long to remain in solitude and when and how to return to the world to serve others. Mechthild poses the question, how should we respond to God's touch? Then she answers with a most profound statement:

> Welcome it. . . . Give it time and room in you; that is all that it asks of you. It shall melt you so deeply into God that you know what his will is concerning how long you should pursue his intense caressing of you, and when and how you should work for sinners . . . and should attend the needs of each and every person.[27]

Personal Response
Drinking from Springs of Living Water

Reflection and Journaling

How would you describe the rhythm of intimate solitude and active service in your life? In what ways are these in proportion to each other, and in what ways are they out of balance?

What bigger portrait of the triune God of Scripture does the paradigm of pouring out and streaming back paint for you?

Scripture

Read afresh the account of Elijah's rhythm of intense ministry, renewing solitude and further ministry in 1 Kings 18–20. How do you relate to Elijah's exhaustion and discouragement in chapter 19? In what ways is God offering you refreshment and renewal as he did to Elijah?

Read Mark 1:29-39. Describe the relationship between Jesus' time with the Father in a solitary place and his ministry to the crowds.

Creativity and Action

How can you strengthen your "flowing out" to others in service? What opportunities do you have to reach out to those around you?

How can you cultivate a deeper connection with the Lord as you "flow back" in time alone with him?

Community

Communities of medieval monks were founded on the rhythm of *ora et labora*—prayer and work. How can you help to establish a similar rhythm in your household or the community of believers to which you belong?

If you are currently not part of a healthy community of believers, can you become part of one near you that maintains an intentional balance of solitude and service?

9

Intimacy with the Lord

Drawing Near as the Brides of Christ

At that time the kingdom of heaven will be like ten virgins who took their lamps and went out to meet the bridegroom. Five of them were foolish and five were wise. The foolish ones took their lamps but did not take any oil with them. The wise, however, took oil in jars along with their lamps. The bridegroom was a long time in coming.

MATTHEW 25:1-5

But after the last day, when God shall hold his festive dinner, one shall seat the brides opposite their Bridegroom and thus shall love come to love, body to soul, and they shall possess full power in eternal glory.

O you charming Lamb and delightful Youth, Jesus, Child of the heavenly Father, when you then rise and pass through all the choirs waving lovingly to the virgins, they shall follow you filled with praise to that most overwhelming place of which I can say no more to anyone. How they shall then entertain themselves with you·and devour your love's desire—that is such intimate sweetness and intense oneness—that I know nothing equal to it.

MECHTHILD OF MAGDEBURG

WHAT DOES SPIRITUAL INTIMACY LOOK LIKE? How do we enter into it? What are the dynamics of such a relationship with God?

These are questions the Beguines explored in their day. These women were in love with Jesus. Not satisfied simply to read about the Lord or hear about him in sermons, they wanted to experience him in their hearts. They longed to encounter him in a way they could feel and touch. Their devotion was warm and tangible, even homespun and earthy. The core of their devotion was an intimate relationship with Christ.

That intimacy was understood primarily in terms of being a bride of Christ. Most of the Beguines had renounced marriage in this life in order to commit themselves wholly to Jesus. They were captivated by this love relationship. Longing to be close to Jesus, they pursued their Savior with all their heart. Understanding their relationship with the Lord in terms of the exclusive bond of marriage, they resonated with the message of bridal spirituality.

BRIDAL SPIRITUALITY

Medieval Christianity brimmed with bridal imagery. A strong current of devotion during this time, bridal spirituality focused on the theme of Christ as the Bridegroom and his people as his bride. As a loving Bridegroom, Christ gave his life for his bride and promised he would come back to receive her for all eternity.

The Beguines were not alone in understanding themselves as brides of Christ. Neither were women the only ones who resonated with this theme. Men recognized themselves as spiritual brides as well. Bernard of Clairvaux's sermons welcomed his monastic brothers to savor romantic intensity with the Lord. Across Europe, monks and canons by the thousands explored what it meant to be Christ's bride.[1] Thus men and women alike personalized the reality of Christ as the heavenly Bridegroom as they realized the closest possible relationship with him.

Bridal imagery also punctuates the pages of Scripture. Throughout the Old Testament Yahweh is portrayed as the husband who loves and protects his people who are his bride. When the Israelites break their covenant with God through idolatry, their unfaithfulness is called adultery. Despite their infidelity, God continually woos his people back to himself and is willing to accept them as if they were an innocent virgin: "Though your sins are like scarlet, they shall be as white as snow" (Isaiah 1:18). Despite their wandering hearts, God remains committed to his people, his beloved bride, and he promises to restore them by his unfailing love.

No longer are you to be named "Forsaken,"
nor your land "Abandoned,"
but you shall be called "My Delight,"
and your land, "The Wedded";
for Yahweh takes delight in you
and your land will have its wedding.

Like a young man marrying a virgin,
so will the one who built you wed you,
and as the bridegroom rejoices in his bride,
so will your God rejoice in you. (Isaiah 62:4-5 JB)

That promise is fulfilled in the New Testament when Jesus identifies himself as the Bridegroom (Matthew 9:15; John 3:29). In Revelation we read about the "wedding supper of the Lamb" being prepared (19:9) and the "new Jerusalem, coming down out of heaven from God, prepared as a bride beautifully dressed for her husband" (21:2). Likewise Ephesians 5:25-27 compares a husband's true love for his wife to Jesus' love for the church as his pure bride, for "Christ loved the church and gave himself up for her to make her holy, cleansing her by the washing with water through the word, and to present her to himself as a radiant church, without stain or wrinkle or any other blemish, but holy and blameless."

The bride being prepared for Christ is the church. By implication, all believers are part of that glorious bride, the body of Christ. It is important to keep in view both the corporate dynamics of this truth—the whole church is Christ's bride—and the personal application—each true believer is invited to share in this bridal experience with the Lord. The Lord pursues each one of us in a unique, individual fashion, and we can appropriate such a love relationship with Jesus in our lives.

NEEDED TODAY

Bridal imagery is difficult for some to relate to, especially men. I understand. As a man and a husband, I know what it is to be a bridegroom standing in front of the church waiting to see my bride come down the aisle. To see myself as a bride is quite another thing. Picturing myself in a white gown does not work! Yet if I am going to be true to the Scripture, I must attempt to bridge that gap and explore the implications of Christ as Bridegroom and we, the church, as his bride.

A revival of bridal spirituality would serve us well today. Many Christians today are seeking spiritual intimacy. We yearn for deep belonging. In our current church culture of never-ending programs and three-step solutions, however, few of us take the time to cultivate that closeness with Christ. The bride-Bridegroom imagery of Scripture directly addresses such hunger, legitimizes it and guides us in our exploration of intimate relations with the Divine.

Furthermore, in the overly eroticized climate of our contemporary world, we often shy away from the love language of the Scriptures. Saturated with stimulating images from the media layered on top of a post-Freudian societal psyche, we often see sexual allusion instead of innocence. But we should not let these preconceptions cause us to avoid the topic of intimacy. Bridal spirituality brings sanity to our sex-crazed frame of mind. It refocuses our attention on the more profound need for genuine relational closeness.

Finally, bridal spirituality includes both the feeling of intimacy and its absence. The life of faith is not one long hug from God where we feel safe and content in his arms. As members of a pampered generation, we need to hear this message. Life has come easy to most of us today, so we have little endurance when disappoint arrives. When Jesus does not fulfill our expectations or immediately meet our emotional needs, we panic! The bridal spirituality of past generations presents this less-than-fun side of relationship. It provides for us a splash of realism, yet extends hope of the Beloved's eventual return.

The Beguines help us unpack the possibilities of such intense imagery. They saw themselves wed to Christ and wanted to articulate the abundance of their desire for him and his love for them. We have much to learn from such believers who were far freer than we are to express their affection for Jesus. They model for us the closest possible communion with Christ.

MENTORED THROUGH THE SONG OF SONGS

Following a long tradition dating back to the first centuries of the church, the Beguines looked to the Song of Songs in the Old Testament as a poetic narrative of the soul's relationship with Christ. "I am my lover's and my lover is mine. . . . His banner over me is love" (Song of Songs 6:3; 2:4). The fathers of the church recognized in the Song of Songs a portrayal of Christ's affectionate love for his bride, the church. During the Middle Ages more commentaries were written on this brief book than any other in the Bible.

The women of the thirteenth century lived and breathed the passages of the Song. Their prose and their poetry are filled with echoes of the bride's desire for her Lover and the Lover's delight in his bride. The pages of their works pulsate with allusions to this vibrant love relationship that is the center of their lives. Using the love story in the Song of Songs as a central paradigm of Christ's love for us, these women invite us into an intimate relationship with the Lord.

The love story in the Song of Songs is a drama in five scenes.

The opening scenes resonate with desire, pursuit and intimacy. The Lover and bride draw close and make a commitment to each other. Like all genuine love relationships, however, the narrative in the Song of Songs is not static. After a misunderstanding, the Lover pulls away and cannot be found. Beside herself, the bride frantically seeks for her Lover and will not be intimidated or consoled until she finds him. When all hope seems lost, he comes to her again. The final scene is the saga's fulfillment. The two are reunited, this time to remain together forever.

Scene 1: Longing to be loved. The opening lines of the Song of Songs exclaim the bride's desire. Love entails longing. In particular, it necessitates the quest for intimacy:

> Let him kiss me with the kisses of his mouth—
>   for your love is more delightful than wine.
> Pleasing is the fragrance of your perfumes;
>   your name is like perfume poured out.
>   No wonder the maidens love you!
> Take me away with you—let us hurry!
>   Let the king bring me into his chambers.
> (Song of Songs 1:1-4)

Perhaps more than any of the Beguines, Mechthild of Magdeburg employs the terminology of marital intimacy to describe our love relationship with Christ. She relates to Jesus on a very tangible level. Because of the incarnation—because he was flesh and blood just like us—it is possible for us to encounter the Lord with all of our senses. Thus Mechthild pictures herself as able to hug Jesus and be close to him: "The humanity of our Lord is an intelligible image of his eternal Godhead, so that we can grasp the Godhead with the humanity and, like the Holy Trinity, enjoy, hug, kiss, and embrace God in an incomprehensible manner."[2]

Mechthild aches to be close to Jesus; she often finds herself yearning for greater intimacy with him as her Lover. Describing herself as "a loving soul that cannot exist without God," she cries:

> Lord, you are my lover,
> My desire,
> My flowing fount,
> My sun;
> And I am your reflection.[3]

Mechthild recognizes that an intimate love relationship with the Lord is available to all believers who are willing to set themselves apart for Christ. Nevertheless, when we are close to the Lord it feels as if we are the only one he loves. Such a sense of being special to the Lord displays the vastness of his love, as Mechthild states: "Every soul that serves God in his favor is his dearest love."[4]

Scene 2: The Bridegroom pursues. The action of the Song of Songs begins in earnest as chapter 2 portrays the Lover leaping across the hills to the one who will be his bride:

> Listen! My lover!
> Look! Here he comes,
> leaping across the mountains,
> bounding over the hill. (Song of Songs 2:8)

When he arrives he extends to her a call. Tenderly and enticingly, he invites her to come away with him and enjoy his presence:

> Arise, my darling,
> my beautiful one, and come with me.
> See! The winter is past;
> the rains are over and gone.
> Flowers appear on the earth;
> the season of singing has come,
> the cooing of doves
> is heard in our land.

> The fig tree forms its early fruit;
>> the blossoming vines spread their fragrance.
> Arise, come, my darling;
>> my beautiful one, come with me. (Song of Songs 2:10-13)

So also begins our relationship with the Lord. He is the great initiator. Our longing love for the Almighty is always a response to his blazing love for us. Our search for him is simply a reflection of his prior pursuit of us. If we are thirsty for the Lord, it is because he is thirsty for our soul. "He is as lovesick for her as he always was," asserts Mechthild, "for he neither increases nor decreases."[5] "God is love," proclaims 1 John 4:8, and that reality never diminishes over time. It is God's love that sets us on fire and makes our souls thirst for him.

When Christ comes, he always extends an invitation to us. Indeed, he calls us each by name. Such is the personal nature of the Lord's love for us. Mechthild highlights the divine initiative in our relationship with Christ. Following the pattern of the Song of Songs, she provides us with dialog between the Lord and the thirsty soul.

[Soul] Ah, Lord, love me passionately, love me often, and love me long. For the more passionately you love me, the purer I shall become. The more often you love me, the more beautiful I shall become. The longer you love me, the holier I shall become here on earth.

[God] That I love you passionately comes from my nature, for I am love itself. That I love you often comes from my desire, for I desire to be loved passionately. That I love you long comes from my being eternal, for I am without an end and without a beginning.[6]

God's love is limitless—it is part of his very nature. God's love is also transformative—it profoundly changes us the closer we draw near to it. As we respond to God's desire for us and embrace his presence and love, we are made purer, lovelier and holier than any effort of our own could effect.

Especially for those who find intimate imagery difficult to personalize, this scene is a good place to commence. We can begin to explore bridal spirituality by reflecting on passages that describe God's initiative toward us, such as "We love because he first loved us" (1 John 4:19). Although we often speak of choosing Christ or accepting him, the reality is that he always takes the first step. When we seek him, it is a response to his initial and eternal love for us, for he is the one who places spiritual hunger and thirst within us.

A passage that captivated me personally for a whole summer is Ephesians 1:4-5. God "chose us in [Christ] before the creation of the world to be holy and blameless in his sight. In love he predestined us to be adopted." As I meditated on these verses my heart opened up. Before creating the universe, he chose me! I am loved. I am pursued.

Another passage expressing God's tender love is Jeremiah 31:3: "I have loved you with an everlasting love," says the Lord. "I have drawn you with loving-kindness." To begin realizing that such love has been poured out toward us since before the foundation of the world is to start opening our hearts to God's initiative and intimacy on a brand new level.

Scene 3: The bride experiences intimacy with the Lover. The Song of Songs progresses with allusions of intimacy:

> I held him and would not let him go
> > till I had brought him to my mother's house,
> > to the room of the one who conceived me.
> (Song of Songs 3:4)

Reflecting such intimacy, Mechthild describes our souls' most tender times with the Lord. Using the language of two people passionately in love with each other, she does not shy away from romantic allusions:

> He greets her in courtly language . . . clothes her in the garments that one fittingly wears in a palace, and surrenders himself into her power. . . . Then he draws her further to a secret place. . . . Then she soars further to a blissful place of which I neither will nor can speak. . . . Yet when infinite God brings the unfathomable soul to the heights, she loses sight of the earth in her astonishment and is not aware of ever having been on earth. [But] just when the game is at its best, one has to leave.[7]

Such intense times with God are available to us, according to the Beguines. Almost in ecstasy, we lose touch with everything around us. We enjoy such closeness with the Lord that we cannot find words to describe it. Yet we cannot stay there for long: just when we relish his presence the most, we come back to ourselves and our earthly existence. It must be that way so long as we live in mortal bodies. Our rapturous times with the Lord are a foretaste of the final banquet in heaven and the full consummation of the marriage between the bride and Christ.

Intimacy, however, can be intimidating. It leaves us vulnerable. As we seek to explore bridal spirituality today, we must admit that we do not like to be defenseless. Contemporary people want to be in charge. Men in particular avoid the threat that emotional vulnerability presents. Likewise, intellectuals tend to avoid the affective side of faith, instead keeping the emphasis on a rational understanding of God. Emotions and language of the heart seem unpredictable and potentially out of control.

Here we can learn from medieval believers. Not only the Beguines but untold numbers of monks and nuns unabashedly pursued intimate encounters with Christ. They were certainly aware of the dangers of overemotionalism and an unbridled emphasis on experience. Yet they call us to take the plunge, as it were, into the deep waters of affectionate love for God.

Mechthild is aware of the hesitance some Christians have toward allowing God to get too close. Rather than busying ourselves with so much activity to keep the Lord at arm's length, we must open ourselves up and allow him to flow to us. Using such bridal language Mechthild calls us to embrace the Lord's most intimate advances and not resist his love, no matter how overwhelming it might be:

> He lives in the peace of holy affection and whispers to his beloved in the narrow confines of the soul. He also embraces her in the noble comfort of his love. He greets her with his loving eyes when they earnestly gaze at one another with love. He kisses her passionately with his divine mouth. . . . Then she rises to the heights of bliss and to the most exquisite pain when she becomes truly intimate with him. Ah, dear Soul, let yourself be loved and don't fiercely fend it off.[8]

Scene 4: The Bridegroom departs. The initial bliss does not continue uninterrupted. As the drama unfolds in the Song of Songs, the bride seems to take her Lover for granted. Rather than responding to his advances, she plays coy—and does so for too long. The Lover leaves her. As soon as he departs, she becomes distraught and fears she has chased him away for good. She calls after him but it is too late, so she runs into the streets seeking the one she loves.

> I opened for my lover,
>> but my lover had left: he was gone.
>> My heart sank at his departure.
> I looked for him but did not find him.
>> I called him but he did not answer.
> The watchmen found me

as they made their rounds in the city.
They beat me, they bruised me. . . .
O daughters of Jerusalem, I charge you—
if you find my lover,
what will you tell him?
Tell him I am faint with love. (Song of Songs 5:6-8)

When the Bridegroom leaves, the bride feels forsaken. Medieval writers call this the "wound of love." She is wounded, or "smitten," in that she is dramatically in love with him and cannot bear to live life without him. In a sense she has also injured him by her resistance. The theme of wounded love was a favorite of the Beguines. Mechthild articulates that wound of love—when we are so stricken that we become lovesick:

Tell my dear Lord Jesus Christ
How sick with love for him I am.
If I am ever to recover,
He himself must be my physician.
Tell him in confidence
The wounds that he has inflicted upon me
I can no longer endure
Unsalved and unbandaged.
He has wounded me to death.
If he leaves me lying here untended,
I can never recover.
If all mountains were a balsam for wounds
And all waters a health potion
And all blossoming trees a bandage to heal wounds,
They could not restore me to health.
He must lay himself onto the wounds of my soul.[9]

How we likewise seek the Lord at times, trying to find where he has gone! Perhaps we have taken his presence in our lives for granted only to realize too late how much we miss our time with him. We long for him and pursue him, knowing that only he himself can heal the wound in our hearts with his loving touch.

Scene 5: They reunite in love. When the sense of the Lord's immediate presence disappears, our souls cry out in anguish, as Mechthild portrays:

> My veins contract
> And my heart melts out of love for you,
> And my soul roars
> With the bellowing of a hungry lion,
> Tell me, dearest One,
> What will it be like for me then,
> And where will you be?[10]

In the midst of her distress, Mechthild hears the reassuring voice of the Lord's response to us:

> You are like a new bride
> Whose one and only lover has slipped away as she slept.
> She had entrusted him with all her love
> And simply cannot endure his parting from her for
>   one hour. . . .
> I come to you at my pleasure, when I will.
> If you are patient and calm,
> And hide your care where you can,
> Then the power of love shall grow in you. . . .
> And I shall be waiting for you in the orchard of love
> And shall pluck for you the flowers of sweet union.[11]

In reality the Bridegroom has not forsaken the bride as she fears. The Song of Songs assures us that he still thinks of her and will soon present himself to her in a tangible way:

> You are beautiful, my darling, as Tirza,
>   lovely as Jerusalem,
>   majestic as troops with banners.

Turn your eyes from me;

they overwhelm me. (Song of Songs 6:4-5)

I have never met a Christian who cannot resonate with a sense of being forgotten by God at some point in his or her life. The poetic imagery in the Song of Songs helps some to describe their experience. Others relate less to the symbolism found in Hebrew verse. In either case the principle is the same: at times we fear we have been abandoned.

Our fear that the Lover has forgotten us is unfounded. He loves us even when we cannot feel his presence as before. He promised, "Never will I leave you; never will I forsake you" (Hebrews 13:5; Deuteronomy 31:6). In time we will realize his presence again and know that we are reunited with him.

INVITATION TO INTIMACY

Living in the imagery of the Song of Songs, the Beguines tapped into streams of bridal spirituality. They also welcomed other women into bridal intimacy with Christ. One beautiful memorial that still stands is the inscription above the gate of the Beguine complex in the city of Diest, Belgium, bidding others to join in the personal relationship that they have encountered with Christ as their Bridegroom. In Dutch their invitation to women reads: "Come into my courtyard, my sister bride."

That invitation has stood through the centuries and still calls believers today to draw near to Christ in bridal intimacy. This is a welcome offer to women and men today who desire above all else to pursue a deeper life with the Lord. Bridal spirituality offers to thirsty believers a love relationship with Jesus and the most intimate friendship with him who is our heavenly Bridegroom.

Personal Response
Drinking from Springs of Living Water

Reflection and Journaling

In what ways do you resonate with bridal spirituality? In what ways is it a stretch for you to relate to this imagery?

What dynamics of the Song of Songs do you relate to most: the Bridegroom's initiation, the exclusive commitment, the Bridegroom's absence or reunited love? What emotion does each of these stages stir inside your heart?

How are you encouraged by the Beguines' uncompromising pursuit of Christ? How do you long for greater intimacy with the Lord?

Scripture

Read Ephesians 5:22-32 and Revelation 19:7-8. What image of Christ as the heavenly Bridegroom do the Scriptures portray?

Read the Song of Songs afresh in light of your love relationship with the Lord. How does the Lover's call to "come away with me, my beautiful one" speak to your heart?

Creativity and Action

On paper or canvas, portray how Christ sees you as his bride. Perhaps you want to create a picture of yourself coming to him as the Bridegroom at the great wedding feast, or maybe you would rather represent yourself as the waiting virgin.

In creative dance recreate the Song of Songs. What movements express your longing for Christ the heavenly Bridegroom?

Community

In a small group, share how Jesus is the deepest love of your life. How are you, like these women of the thirteenth century, willing to set out into un-charted waters in your pursuit of Jesus?

Find a friend you can talk to about your intimate relationship with Christ. Not everyone understands the language of the heart, but if you look carefully you will find a confidant whom you can tell about your deepest affections for Jesus.

10

Transformation Through Trials

Mechthild Summons Us to Embrace Suffering

Consider it pure joy, my brothers and sisters, whenever you face trials of many kinds, because you know that the testing of your faith produces perseverance. Let perseverance finish its work so that you may be mature and complete, not lacking anything.

JAMES 1:2-4 (TNIV)

Constant longing in the soul,
Constant days of pain in the body,
Constant anguish in the senses,
Constant hope in one's heart for no one but Jesus—
All who have forsaken themselves in God
Know well what I am saying.

MECHTHILD OF MAGDEBURG

WHEN MECHTHILD WAS SIXTY-THREE YEARS OLD, she transferred to a Benedictine convent at Helfta, Germany, where she spent the last twelve years of her life. Part of the Cistercian revival sweeping Europe, Helfta beamed with spiritual vitality. Home to other spiritual writers like Gertrude the Great and Mechthild of Hackeborn—each of whom wrote well-known works on the spiritual life—this convent was a notable center for spiritual formation. Even so, the nuns appreciated Mechthild's spiritual depth and sought counsel from her. It was at Helfta that Mechthild penned the seventh and final book of her spiritual classic *Flowing Light of the Godhead.*

A well-to-do convent, Helfta offered Mechthild a life of reasonable comfort, security and care as younger sisters nursed her in her old age. Despite such physical succor, these last years were marked with suffering for Mechthild. Some of the pain she experienced came from inner turmoil. Although the nuns of Helfta welcomed Mechthild, she was always aware that she was not on the same social plane as they. Helfta was home to women from prominent noble families, and many of the sisters were able to read and write in Latin. Although the nuns received Mechthild with open arms and respected her spiritual counsel, the former Beguine was perennially conscious that she came from a lower class.

Mechthild endured an even greater amount of pain from aging. Eventually she lost her eyesight and the ability to clothe herself. She felt humiliated by her need to have a younger sister nurse her and clean her. Yet she sought to thank God in all her circumstances:

Lord, I thank you for taking from me my eyesight and for now serving me with the eyes of others.

Lord, I thank you for taking from me the use of my hands and for now serving me with the hands of others.

Lord, I thank you for taking from me the strength of my heart and for now serving me with the hearts of others.

Lord, on their behalf, I beg you to reward them on earth with your divine love.[1]

Unlike now, when we have powerful drugs to administer to those who are dying, people in the Middle Ages often endured unrelenting torment. The last weeks of life were commonly referred to as the "final agony" because of the torturous nature of death. Mechthild endured just such suffering in her last months. But on her deathbed she continued to surrender herself to God. She was ready to die and be with the Lord, yet even in her great distress she desired only to see God's will accomplished and his name glorified:

> For two days and two nights I was so seriously ill that I had hope that my end had come. . . . I urged God to take me to him if that were his dearest will. "And yet, Lord, if your praise can at all be increased thereby, I shall gladly remain in this miserable body for love of you. Lord, I have so lived for many a day that, Lord, I never offered you such a difficult sacrifice as this. Lord, thy will be done and not mine. I do not have dominion over myself. You do in all things."[2]

Such was the complete embrace of suffering that Mechthild cultivated her whole life. Remaining thankful to God while she was in such agony was the most costly sacrifice she ever made; nevertheless, she abandoned herself to God's plan, willing to enter eternal rest or to continue in earthly torment.

AFRAID OF SUFFERING

Our contemporary culture recoils from suffering in any form. We fear pain. We avoid distress at all cost. We supply ample medication for anyone in anguish. Often we send the terminally ill away where we cannot see their agony.

Pain and suffering, however, are part and parcel of life. Every child is brought into this world through the intense distress of delivery. Growing pains accompany physical, intellectual and social development. The process of aging and death is filled with grief. Even our deep longing for the Lord can cause excruciating inner anguish.

Ironically, the one arena where we recognize the reality of pain and openly allow it is sports. Here we embrace the motto "No pain, no gain." The fact that pain is acceptable in athletics should grab our attention. The reality is that suffering is not the worst thing in life. It can be endured and even embraced when it leads to a greater good. Athletes ignore screaming pain while playing a sport simply because they enjoy the game. Many of us transcend substantial pain at the gym for the fleeting vanity of a slimmer waistline. In the same manner we can face life's suffering without fear if we can grasp the bigger picture.

We grow through pain. In particular, we mature spiritually through trials and tribulations. If we can reimage our suffering as part of the growth process, our fear of pain begins to dissipate. We transcend the immediate misery—real as it may be—because we see the glorious end that it will bear. Mechthild helps guide us in this process. From the deep well of her personal experience, she has much to mentor us with regarding the role of affliction and pain in our spiritual formation.

SHARING IN HIS SUFFERING

The whole of the New Testament calls us to participate in Jesus' life, affliction, death and resurrection. Much more than "getting saved," true faith is identifying with Christ. A central element of being united with Christ is sharing in his suffering. For the believer, suffering is not simply about pain—it is joining in Jesus' passion.

Our Lord said that to be his disciple would mean crucifixion: "Anyone who does not carry his cross and follow me cannot be my disciple" (Luke 14:27). Mechthild spells out our Lord's command to take up our cross daily:

So, follow me! You shall be martyred with me, betrayed in jealousy, hunted in ambush, taken prisoner in hate, bound in obedience, . . . slapped by the rage of the world, brought to trial in confession, . . . stripped naked by abandonment, scourged by poverty, crowned with trails, spat upon by disgrace, bearing your cross in the hatred of sin, . . . wounded by love, dying on the cross in holy constancy, . . . buried in oblivion, arisen from the dead in a holy end, and drawn up into heaven in God's breath.[3]

Enduring trials and tribulations is a form of participation with the Lord. The apostle Paul emphasizes such union with Christ in his suffering: "I want to know Christ and the power of his resurrection and the fellowship of sharing in his sufferings, becoming like him in his death" (Philippians 3:10). Paul wants to take part in Jesus' passion. He understands a truth that is virtually forgotten in the church today: a key component of being identified with the Lord is sharing in his suffering. In line with Paul's thoughts, Mechthild pictures the Lord saying to her:

I was nailed to the cross with them; for this reason they should suffer willingly and complain little about their troubles.

I entrusted my spirit with them to my Father at my death; thus should they entrust themselves to me in all their trials.[4]

We participate with Christ by being crucified with him. "I have been crucified with Christ," proclaims Paul in Galatians 2:20, "and I no longer live, but Christ lives in me." Mechthild fleshes out the implications of being crucified with Christ in book 3 of her *Flowing Light*. In a beautiful passage, she places herself along with our Lord in each scene of his passion:

She is sent to Herod. . . .
She is delivered up to Pilate again. . . .
She carries her cross on a sweet path
When she truly surrenders herself to God in all sufferings. . . .
She suffers terrible thirst on the cross of love as well. . . .

But they all come thronging and offer her gall. . . .
Then in a holy ending she is taken from her cross
And speaks: "Father, receive my spirit; now everything
    is [complete]."[5]

When we embrace suffering in this life, we join in Christ's suffering. Medieval believers referred to this as the *imitatio Christi*, the imitation of Christ. By this phrase they implied not so much that we try to do what Jesus might have done—for by our own strength we are unable to act like Christ. Rather, *imitatio Christi* means to follow in Christ's footsteps, to be identified with him and especially to join in his passion. "But if you suffer for doing good and you endure it, this is commendable before God," writes Peter in his first epistle. "To this you were called, because Christ suffered for you, leaving you an example, that you should follow in his steps" (1 Peter 2:20-21).

SUFFERING ENNOBLED

When we see our pain as participation in Christ's pain, it transforms our suffering. As Mechthild asserts, "Through the noble struggle of our Lord and through his holy suffering our Christian struggle and our suffering, accepted in good spirit, are ennobled and made holy."[6]

If we share in Christ's suffering, we will also share in his glory. Peter tells us that "now for a little while you may have had to suffer grief in all kinds of trials" (1 Peter 1:6). In this life we indeed face all varieties of trials and tribulations. However, Peter exhorts us not to be caught off guard when such difficulties come our way but to joy in the coming glory we will experience. "Dear friends, do not be surprised at the painful trial you are suffering, as though something strange were happening to you. But rejoice that you participate in the sufferings of Christ, so that you may be overjoyed when his glory is revealed" (I Peter 4:12-13; see also Romans 8:18).

Mechthild is ever conscious of this link between suffering and glory. Indeed it empowers her during the most difficult times. That divine glory will shine through us, she affirms: "To the degree that we accept our suffering with gratitude here and bear it with patience, God's holy suffering shall light up and shine in our suffering."[7]

OUR DESIRES PURIFIED THROUGH SUFFERING

Although we often claim to love the Lord with our whole heart, our pledge to him is frequently more fickle than we care to admit. Certainly we love Jesus, but we also love many other things. If we are not careful, the pleasure of possessions and pride and popularity can draw our hearts away from our first love. Thus we need to direct our hearts toward the Lord and away from all the false lovers that seek our attention.

No one matures spiritually except the one "who has removed himself from all consolation and all favors in this world," Mechthild writes. She cuts to the heart of the matter: "For pleasure has cut us off from God. And so we must return to him through suffering."[8] God, therefore, takes away the delights we have in many earthly things so that we begin to thirst for spiritual realities that will truly fulfill us. "Just so does our Lord cast his chosen friends far from earthly consolation, so that they might hunger for heavenly consolation."[9] Those who earnestly love the Lord focus their desire on him alone.

In order to have our desires purified, we need to welcome the trials God sends instead of complaining about the discomfort they cause us. "Consider it pure joy . . . whenever you face trials of many kinds," challenges James in the opening verses of his epistle (James 1:2). Mechthild brings this point home for our lives:

Whoever in pain complains of his burdens
Is either blind in knowledge

Or spineless in forbearance.
His love has grown cold.[10]

Life provides plenty of sorrow. The Beguine from Magdeburg exhorts us as her readers to accept the trials the Lord allows in our lives. She notes that "suffering is much nobler and more useful which God inflicts upon us," whether it comes via persecution by God's enemies or mistreatment by other Christians. The issue is that God has a purpose for that suffering in our lives and he is "nobler than all tormentors," whether they are friends or enemies.[11] Rather than removing us from our current situation, God allows us to grow through the circumstances where he has placed us. Life on earth is an intensive preparation. According to Mechthild, the Lord's will is

To let you remain in earthly misery
Until all my sweetness rises up
To the heights of eternal glory,
And my strings shall play sweetly for you
In tune with the true value of your patient love.
Still, before I begin,
I want to tune my heavenly strings in your soul,
So that you might persevere even longer.
For well-born brides and noble knights
Must undergo a long and intensive preparation at
    great cost.[12]

EMBRACING SUFFERING

Although life provides ample suffering of all kinds—physical, emotional, relational—the experience of pain by itself does not automatically cause spiritual growth. We must embrace the trials God allows in our lives if we are to benefit from them. We must make a conscious choice to accept that suffering, no matter its source, so that we can grow.

Suffering is painful by its very definition. Yet we can be joyful in the midst of it. Such joy comes from recognizing the end result of our tribulations. Like James, the apostle Paul emphasizes the outcome of our sorrows: "But we also rejoice in our sufferings, because we know that suffering produces perseverance; perseverance, character; and character, hope" (Romans 5:3-4).

Therefore we can be joyful even in the midst of distress, as Mechthild states: "God guides his chosen children along strange paths. This is a strange path and a noble path and a holy path that God himself trod: . . . [enduring] pain. Upon this path the soul that aches for God is joyful, for by nature she is joyful to her Lord, who suffered much pain because of his good deeds."[13]

In order to help us endure tribulation and accept God's work in our lives Mechthild offers us her homespun recipe to help us swallow the unpleasant medicine:

> Suffering is bitter. And so we grind up a spice called "willingly suffer." A second spice is called "patience in suffering." It is also bitter. And so to counter it we grind up another spice called "holy intimacy," which turns patience sweet, as well as all our hard work. A third spice is "to persevere long in suffering," waiting for our eternal life and salvation. This is also very bitter. And so to counter this we grind up a spice called "with joy unflagging." . . . After a bitter potion one is certainly in need of tasty food. Rising desire and sinking humility and flowing love—these three maidens bring the soul up to heaven before God.[14]

Clear evidence that we have begun to welcome God's plan for our lives—with all the pain and trials it entails—is that we worship the Almighty in the midst of affliction. It is easy to express thanks to the Lord when things are going well; it is quite a different thing to glorify God when we find ourselves in trying times, physically or spiritually. The praise that is most valuable—that costs us the most—is that which is done when we are in pain. Mechthild describes such an offering of worship when "one is willing, able, and skillful in praising God well from the heart and in thanking him cheerfully and in raising one's desires aloft and in bringing one's works to fruition while one is in poverty, in disgrace, in loneliness, in times of suffering, in spiritual aridity." Glorifying God during spiritually dry times, she says, is the most difficult of all, especially when we are experiencing "all kinds of bitterness both within and without."[15]

We will know that we have truly embraced God's work in us when it makes no difference to us whether he brings suffering or consolation. They become all the same to us.

So, too, those whom I draw to myself on earth
Suffer much pain because of it.
They should indeed know this:
The harder I draw them toward me,
The nearer they come to me.
When a person so overcomes himself
That he considers suffering and consolation of equal value,
Then I shall raise him up into sweetness,
And thus he shall have a taste of eternal life.[16]

COMING INTO MATURITY

Suffering is not a way to earn merit or win God's favor. We can never warrant God's love or work our way to greater reward. Nevertheless, pain is a common means by which God works in our lives. In experiences of suffering and frustration, God matures us in the most profound ways.

God's design through our affliction is for us to come into intimate fellowship with him. Much like Hadewijch, Mechthild describes her walk with God in terms of a progression toward a mature marriage union. It begins with youthful romance, but over the years the intense emotions and spiritual sweetness settle down into the common reality of daily married life. In the final book of *Flowing Light*, the Lord declares to her:

> Your childhood was a playmate of my Holy Spirit.
> Your youth was a bride of my humanity.
> Your old age is now a housewife of my Godhead.[17]

Such is the normal development of spiritual maturity. Through the vicissitudes of life there is an overarching progression. We begin with the thrill of a newfound best Friend. That friendship grows in intimacy as we seek greater depth and as we burn with passionate desire for more of the Lord. Then we move through the agony of searching love when the Lord seems far away and we feel dry and destitute. If we persevere, though, we ultimately come into the security of a settled relationship, like that of a long, stable marriage. There we experience a quiet, peaceful assurance of his love that cannot be shaken.

Embracing suffering does not mean we are demeaned, but Mechthild is honest enough to tell us that it certainly seems that way at times. When we go through trials, it feels as if the Lord has given us a "wretched box on the ears." More than that, Mechthild states outright that it makes her "seem so worthless." Discipline is never enjoyable in the short run, but God uses it to bring us to a new place of glory. Thus Mechthild assures us that God promises victory beyond all our trials, and he calls us into intimate love with himself:

> Your mountain shall dissolve in love;
> Your enemies shall gain no part of you . . .
> And in my kingdom you shall be a new bride;
> And there I shall give you a delicious kiss on the mouth,
> That my entire Godhead shall soar through your soul . . .
> So where is your grieving now?[18]

Far from viewing us as valueless, God sees us as his beautiful, beloved bride. As we receive his kiss, all of the former pain and sorrow vanish. Such an ending makes all of the pain worthwhile. When we ultimately pass into eternity, we will come into God's "glorious palace in which God eternal shall caress his love-starved bride without end with all the pleasure in his power according to her consuming desire."[19]

MENTORED BY MECHTHILD

When we think about aids to spiritual growth, suffering is not usually the first theme that comes to mind. In fact we generally view suffering and spiritual well-being as polar opposites. To the contrary, Mechthild and her fellow medieval believers recognized trials as unique opportunities to grow spiritually. Christians in this bygone era sought to embrace pain and tribulation as part of God's good plan in their lives. Physical affliction was as awful for them as it is for us. They endured mental illness, psychological suffering and the inner pain of relational conflict as we do. In addition, grief from the untimely death of family members was far more common than today. Yet they viewed all of life's events as occasions for spiritual formation.

The German Beguine, therefore, guides us along the painful path of sharing in Christ's suffering. She assures us that God does his deepest work in our hearts through the most painful times. Much spiritual growth comes about by the trials and tribulations we endure. From the first delights of entering into a relationship with the Divine through long years of walking with him in the day-in and day-out of our lives, suffering is integral to the process of maturity. The key, Mechthild says, is to embrace God's will—no matter how difficult or sorrowful. She shows us the bigger picture that helps us transcend pain and reminds us to receive all things from the Lord:

I know this for certain: that no matter what the friends of God suffer, God never forgets them, for he is their help and their consolation in all their troubles. We should fight on accordingly, and suffer willingly in joy. Then we shall sparkle and shine in the sight of God.[20]

Personal Response
Drinking from Springs of Living Water

Reflection and Journaling

How do you long deeply for the Lord? How is your longing a burning desire similar to Mechthild's passion for Jesus? In what ways could you describe that yearning as an ache in your heart?

What are some areas of pain or trial in your life? How can you consider these as "pure joy," as James exhorts? In what ways are they developing endurance in your life and making you mature and complete?

Scripture

Read Romans 8 with fresh eyes to see the integral connection between suffering (especially verses 18 and 35-36) and being conformed into the image of Christ (verses 28-30). What statement is the apostle Paul making in this chapter?

Read the book of 1 Peter and underline every reference to trial or suffering. What can be included in Peter's "all kinds of trials" (4:12)? How does Peter connect present suffering with eternal glory?

Creativity and Action

If you are artistically inclined, express suffering through art, writing or dance. Is there a way you can depict your own suffering as a participation in Christ's passion? Or can you somehow portray the glorious outcome of your present heartache?

Community

If you have suffered—or are currently suffering—you will quickly be able to recognize those around you who are in pain. Talk to someone who is suffering and be a listening ear for them. If the time is right, share a verse or two on suffering that might encourage them and help them see the bigger picture of what God is shaping in their lives.

11

Beautiful Life of Freedom

Devout Women Share Their Secret of Dying to Self

Very truly I tell you, unless a kernel of wheat falls to the ground and dies, it remains only a single seed. But if it dies, it produces many seeds. Those who love their life will lose it, while those who hate their life in this world will keep it for eternal life.

JOHN 12:24-25 (TNIV)

For the most beautiful life I know . . .
Would be the one in which we let God freely act
In taking or in giving, in storm or in peace, . . .
In which all events would be rated just alike;
If God willed to come, or if he willed to go,
We should understand it all in love,
And see that he himself is Love.

HADEWIJCH OF BRABANT

WE DREAM OF A LIFE OF FREEDOM. We long to experience the beautiful life of abundance that Jesus promised. Our hearts resonate with the apostle Paul's promise in Galatians 5:1: "It is for freedom that Christ set you free." However, inner freedom comes at a price.

To arrive at that beautiful place, as Hadewijch describes it, we must let go of our agenda—we must die to our self-will. Indeed, the Christian life is all about dying to self. That is the gospel: through death we are resurrected into new life. As we let go of our agenda, we begin to grasp God's.

Dying to our will is a long, painful process. What's more, it runs counter to today's climate of self-realization. Contemporary Western society is obsessed with self. Self-expression is seen as the highest good. The quest for self-identity lays the foundation for the world around us. Unbridled egoism encourages everyone to "strut their stuff" and always "look out for number one." In our day, people are willing to sacrifice time with family, friends and the Lord on the altar of self-achievement. Our current culture values self-fulfillment above all else.

Many Christians today have become accustomed to the mindset of self. Far more influenced by our surrounding culture than we realize, twenty-first-century Christians are fascinated with self-fulfillment. Even our teaching on the Spirit's gifts and our emphasis on leadership resound with self-will. Rather than seeking opportunities to serve, we are motivated to use spiritual gifts in pursuit of self-actualization.

Much ministry is accomplished out of self-expression and the will to power. In his book *Absolute Surrender*, Andrew Murray observes how those in Christian ministry "pray for power for work, and power for blessing, but they have not prayed for power for full deliverance from self."[1] A. W. Tozer echoes such concerns in his classic *The Pursuit of God*: "Promoting self under the guise of promoting Christ is currently so common as to excite little notice."[2] Often the motivation of our heart is mixed. On one hand we desire to serve God; on the other, with an often unconscious drive to achieve, we move forward with our own plans and willpower. In doing so, we fail to follow Jesus' example. Although the second person of the Trinity, Christ refrained from launching out on his own initiative while on earth. "I tell you the truth, the Son can do nothing by himself; he can do only what he sees his Father doing, because whatever the Father does the Son also does" (John 5:19; see also 5:30; 6:38; 8:28; 12:49; and 14:10).

DYING TO SELF

Because of the fall, our self-nature is bent in on itself. Yet on our own we cannot see our error—we are deceived. We lack the perspective necessary to see our own self-orientation. Whether it manifests as selfishness, self-will, self-exaltation or self-hatred, a fundamental self-absorption underlies our human nature.

Cutting across the grain of humanity's obsession with self, Christ calls us to "come and die."[3] Central to the Christian gospel is the message of the cross. In order for us to receive the new life Jesus offers, we must abandon our self-directed existence. "If anyone would come after me," states Jesus, "he must deny himself and take up his cross and follow me. For whoever wants to save his life will lose it, but whoever loses his life for me will save it" (Luke 9:23-24). In order to be true followers of Christ, we must release the grip we maintain on our lives, forsaking our self-life and surrendering completely to God's sovereign care.

Even when we deeply desire to grow in the Lord, it is difficult to identify our own self-referenced habits. Self-orientation is subtle. We are our own blind spots. Without God's help we cannot even see our self-absorption. Self-sins such as "self-righteousness, self-pity, self-confidence, self-sufficiency, self-admiration, self-love and a host of others like them," writes Tozer, "dwell too deep within us and are too much a part of our natures to come to our attention till the light of God is focused upon them." Yet if we do not address issues of self, we block not only spiritual growth but also our very relationship with God. "Self," continues Tozer, "is the opaque veil that hides the face of God from us."[4]

Dying is never pretty. If you have ever watched an animal die, you know that it often entails a writhing struggle. Yet die we must. "We dare not rest content with a neat doctrine of self-crucifixion," notes Tozer. Rather, we welcome the circumstances God brings into our lives as opportunities to die. By doing so, we realize the cross. As Tozer insists, "The cross is rough and it is deadly, but it is effective."[5]

BEGUINES MODEL DYING

Many of the Beguines knew such dying. Their lives demonstrate for us what spiritual formation looks like free from the self-centered milieu in which we live. They abandoned a comfortable life by choosing a simple existence in the beguinage, giving what little money they had to the poor. Many risked their own lives as they tended the sick and dying. Some endured slander as townspeople shunned them for not marrying and living "normal lives." Others were persecuted for being too radical in their faith.

Not everyone appreciated Mechthild's teaching on spiritual growth, and some outright opposed her for writing her *Flowing Light of the Godhead*. Medieval society in general—and church officials in particular—held suspect women who composed books, especially on theological topics. "I was warned against writing this book," she wrote. "It could be burned."[6] Despite the danger of being censured, however, Mechthild penned her experiences and instructed others in spiritual formation, knowing that God had called her. She likely received some protection from suspicion by joining the established convent at Helfta.

Hadewijch did not fare as well in the latter days of her life. For some years she had served as the mistress of her Beguine community, most likely in Antwerp. Although her leadership was welcomed at first, in time the women challenged her authority. It seems that her zeal for spiritual growth was too extreme for the other Beguines and they resisted her call for total commitment to Christ. Due to this opposition Hadewijch was ousted from the community and wandered the remainder of her life exiled and homeless. Scholars believe she was likely pursued by the Inquisition, since by the late thirteenth century suspicion of heresy had fallen on the Beguines, especially those who were not members of an established household.

In this dire situation, Hadewijch trusted that "in all things God works for the good of those who love him, who have been called according to his purpose" (Romans 8:28). "What happens to me," states Hadewijch in a letter to a one of the Beguines she had mentored, "whether I am wandering in the country or put in prison—however it turns out, it is the work of Love."[7]

INSIGHTS

In their writings the Beguines shine a light of freedom into our self-absorbed prison. Both Hadewijch and Mechthild are brutally honest in facing their fallen selves. They recognize that spiritual formation is all about dying to self. Emphasizing the cross, they help us identify our own self-orientation. Moreover, they invite us to die to ourselves so that we can enter into full, intimate relationship with Christ.

Hadewijch pens a letter of instruction to a dear sister who is overly busy with ministry and service to others. While Hadewijch appreciates her desire to serve, she encourages this younger Beguine to do so in a manner that maintains her inner peace, rather than hastily immersing herself into every opportunity that presents itself:

> O dear love . . . you busy yourself unduly with many things, and so many of them are not suited to you. You waste too much time with your energy, throwing yourself headlong into the things that cross your path. I could not persuade you to observe moderation in this. When you want to do something, you always plunge into it as if you could pay heed

to nothing else. It pleases me that you comfort and help all your friends, yes, the more the better—provided you and they remain in peace; I willingly allow that.[8]

In order to love someone, we must forget ourselves and turn our attention to the other. So it is with the Lord: we need to relinquish our self-referenced way of life and abandon ourselves to Love incarnate. Hadewijch writes:

> He who wishes to win victories in love
> Must . . . in accordance with Love's deserts, renounce the
>   whole of himself,
> And with her condemn or bless
> Both himself and what he hates and loves.
> All the right he has he so gives over to Love
> That he wishes nothing, and Love does not need
> To refuse him anything she gives him. . . .
> Desire cuts, as it were, an abyss in him;
> So Love must fill it completely.
> Alas, how entirely must anyone forsake himself
> When he wholly gives himself up to Love.[9]

DYING TO OUR OWN AGENDA

As we embrace the struggles of life, we die to our will and our timetable. If we truly want to grow in the Lord, we must allow our own agenda to be crucified in order for God's will to become our own. Although as believers we generally assume our plans are altruistic and presume that they must also be God's program for our lives, our agendas are regularly tainted by self—that is part of our fallen condition. "God's will is pure," notes Mechthild; "our will is very much contaminated by the flesh."[10]

In like manner Hadewijch exposes self-will:

> People preconceive themselves to be led by the Spirit,
> When it is chiefly their own will.

Again, something that ruins them
They think is consolation and comes from God.[11]

Along with our desires, our prayers can be shallow and self-serving. Just because we want something does not mean the Lord has placed that desire within us. "You do not have, because you do not ask God," asserts James as he writes to Christians. "When you ask, you do not receive, because you ask with wrong motives, that you may spend what you get on your pleasures" (James 4:2-3).

Many times we are sad in life simply because we do not get our own way. Not satisfied with the circumstances in which God has placed us, we demand our own will and sulk when the Lord does not give it to us. Mechthild recognizes that as believers we will be sullen as long as we try to hold onto our own will. It is when we release our agenda to the Lord that we experience true freedom and joy in this life. "The greatest joy in heaven is the will of God. When unwillingness becomes willingness, God's joy enters into the heart of a sad person. . . . We should accept gifts of pain with joy. We should accept gifts of comfort with fear. Thus we can put all things that come our way to good use. Dear friend, be in harmony with God, and be happy with his will."[12]

Therefore, we must offer our will to the Lord and never take it back. Mechthild prays for God's grace to yield her will to his: "Help me also, Lord, to keep you by giving up completely my own will according to your desire," she cries. "Then I would never, ever lose that love that never ceases to burn. Amen."[13] Only when we have died to self and all the misdirected desires of our old nature do we long for the only One who can satisfy our hearts' deepest dreams. "Nothing tastes good to me but God alone; I am wondrously dead."[14]

"Love is honored [when we live] without other intention than to render Love her proper place," contends Hadewijch. "This is to be crucified with Christ (Gal. 2:19), to die with him, and to rise again with him (Col. 3:1). To this end he must always help us."[15]

LIMITATIONS OF SPIRITUAL DISCIPLINES

At some point all serious Christians face the question, how do I die to myself? In practical terms, how do I "put to death" all that belongs to my "earthly nature" (Colossians 3:5)? Many medieval women and men attempted to answer these questions by practicing vigorous spiritual exercises. They flung themselves into daily Bible reading, memorization and meditation. They fasted for days and prayed all night long. In an attempt to overcome the self-nature and desires of the flesh, more than a few monastics of the age broke their health. Some beat their bodies and even mutilated themselves in an effort to subdue carnal desires and sanctify themselves through their asceticism. Yet they found that such practices often kept their focus back on their own self-sins and self-efforts to overcome them.

Mechthild spoke out against the ascetic severity of her time, no matter how spiritual it may have seemed. At an earlier point in her life, Mechthild had broken her own health with such severity, and she recognized the inadequacy of acute asceticism, counseling others to avoid it. Her interest, however, was not to protect the physical health of the women who practiced such heroics but rather to promote their spiritual well-being.

The problem with spiritual disciplines, notes Mechthild, is that they can be motivated by self-achievement and carried out by self-will. Rather than aiding our spiritual progress, they simply feed the self-life, which is the antithesis of spiritual growth. "They make great fools of themselves who imagine that they are scaling the heights with loathsome, inhuman toils," she asserts, because "their hearts are full of rancor. They are entirely lacking in holy, humble virtues that guide the soul to God. False holiness likes to hide where self-will holds sway in a heart."[16]

Following Augustine and Bernard of Clairvaux, Mechthild makes it clear that human effort can never save us or sanctify us: God by God's grace must do the work in our lives. Our self-motivated spiritual exercises are ineffective in overcoming the self-life of the flesh. While these practices have "an appearance of wisdom, with their self-imposed worship, their false humility and their harsh treatment of the body," Paul says, "they lack any value in restraining sensual indulgence" (Colossians 2:23). Our self-determined disciplines are, by definition, powerless to address the core issue of our fallen nature: self-centeredness.

Trying to guide our own formation via self-selected spiritual exercises leaves us trapped with self. While we may excel in given disciplines that come easily for us, we neglect issues that most need attention. We may savor solitude and even Scripture memorization but refuse to practice patience and humility. We shine in our favorite spiritual practices while we completely miss the inner transformation needed in our lives.[17] In our self-improvement mindset, we adopt various disciplines and go into a regimen of training; however, rather than realizing God's grace in our lives, we become like the Pharisees. Our very success in the practice of spiritual exercises leads to pride and self-righteousness—the most toxic forms of self-absorption.

Self is a pool of quicksand. The more we try to escape through our self-analysis and self-effort, the deeper we sink in the pit of self. The only way we can escape is if someone from the outside throws us a rope. That someone is God. Only God can rescue us—this is what grace is all about.

Divine grace, however, often comes disguised under the cloak of suffering and sorrow. Tribulation is what the Lord generally uses to transform us from self-focus to genuine God-focus and other-focus. Instead of self-determined spiritual exercises, the Beguine women assure us that spiritual maturity comes primarily by embracing life's trials.

INNER REST AND DIVINE INTIMACY

If we die to our agenda and take on the Almighty's, we will come into a place of inner rest and genuine intimacy with God. Our will is not destroyed; rather, it is shaped to fit with God's. As human beings we are volitional creatures, yet the closer we draw to the Lord, the more our wills are transformed to pulsate in perfect harmony with his plans and purposes for us. In order to progress on the path of spiritual growth, Mechthild asserts that we need to surrender our will in three ways. To mature, it is necessary "first, that one submit to God relinquishing all human control. . . . The second thing keeping a person on this path is that one welcome all things except for sin alone. The third thing keeping a person on this path is that one do all things equally for God's honor."[18]

Jesus is our great exemplar. In the garden of Gethsemane our Lord expresses his desire—that he not have to endure the suffering that stands before him. Yet he lays down his agenda and surrenders to the Father: "My Father, if it is possible, may this cup be taken from me. Yet not as I will, but as you will. . . . May your will be done" (Matthew 26:39, 42). Jesus is clearly struggling in the garden; Matthew informs us that our Lord prays this way three times. Like Jesus in Gethsemane, are we willing to lay down our own agenda—our will—in order to fit into God the Father's plan, no matter the cost?

When we allow God to be God, we recognize his right to act as he desires in all things. As sovereign, he is free to do as his unsearchable wisdom dictates. For our part, we learn to rejoice in all situations. As we rejoice and exercise forbearance, the peace that passes all understanding begins to guard our hearts and our minds (Philippians 4:4-7). When we trust in the Lord's faithfulness, we are able to be at rest.

Embracing God's will in all things is the sure path to genuine satisfaction in the Christian life. Whether that entails our welcoming of circumstances or our acceptance of trials with long-suffering, we must cultivate contentment. "I have learned to be content whatever the circumstances," continues the apostle Paul in Philippians 4:11-12. "I know what it is to be in need, and I know what it is to have plenty. I have learned the secret of being content in any and every situation, whether well fed or hungry, whether living in plenty or in want." In like fashion Hadewijch exclaims:

> Oh! If anyone thus totally loves the will of Love—
> In mounting tumult, in lowly silence,
> Through everything Love ever inflicts on him—
> In him Love ever has her fullest contentment.[19]

When Love triumphs over us, we no longer need to be afraid. We let go of our cravings and our fearful self-focus because "there is no fear in love," as 1 John 4:18 assures us: "But perfect love drives out fear." Although we do not understand why God sometimes gives and other times takes away, we have confidence that it all flows from his good will toward us because "God is love" (1 John 4:8). When we rest in God, we are able to release our anxious agenda and our willful self-preservation, assures Hadewijch:

> For when the soul has nothing else but God, and when it retains no will but lives exclusively according to his will alone; and when the soul is brought to naught and with God's will wills all that he wills, and is engulfed in him . . . then he is exalted above the earth, and then he draws all things to him; and so the soul becomes with him all that he himself is.[20]

Beyond the yearning and searching and clamoring of our spiritual pilgrimage, there is a beautiful place of rest. There we can silently enjoy the presence of the Lord with effortless pleasure. That freedom and intimacy come, however, only as our will yields to the Lord's so that there is but a "single will" in the relationship.

Personal Response
Drinking from Springs of Living Water

Reflection and Journaling

In what ways have you seen self-will surface in your practice of spiritual disciplines? How has self-fulfillment tainted any service or ministry in which you are engaged?

Are there ways you thought you were being led by the Spirit in the past that you now recognize to be more your own desire and will at work? How do you desire to develop one will with the Father as Jesus had while on earth?

Scripture

Read the whole of Luke 9 in which Jesus calls us to count the cost of following him. What are the implications of "taking up your cross daily" in your life right now?

Read John 5:19, 30; 6:38; 8:28, 42; 12:49 and 14:10. Jesus says he can do "nothing of himself" but only what he sees and hears the Father doing. Using the exact same phrase, Jesus says we can do "nothing of ourselves" but rather must abide in him as the branch abides in the vine (John 15:1-8). What are the implications of these verses for your life?

Creativity and Action

Try your hand at some poetry as did the Beguines. Hadewijch's writing is refined and structured yet expresses her heart's deepest cries. Mechthild's work is less polished, and she often goes back and forth between poetry and prose. However they emerge, put some of your reflections or prayers down on paper.

Community

Ask a prayer partner or someone in your small group to point out blind spots and self-focus in your life. Although receiving such input will be painful, it will also be healing. In what ways are you ready—or not ready—to invite someone into your life on this level?

12

Lost in God's Love

The Beguines Welcome Us into the Divine Depths

Oh, the depth of the riches of the wisdom and knowledge of God!
How unsearchable his judgments,
and his paths beyond tracing out!
Who has known the mind of the Lord?
Or who has been his counselor?
Who has ever given to God,
that God should repay him?
For from him and through him and to him are all things.
To him be the glory forever! Amen.

—ROMANS 11:33-36

What is sweetest in Love is her tempestuousness;
Her deepest abyss is her most beautiful form;
To lose one's way in her is to touch her close at hand; . . .
Her highest being drowns us in the depths.

—HADEWIJCH OF BRABANT

THE WOMEN OF THE THIRTEENTH CENTURY invite us to sink into God's divine depths. As in the immortal words of Fanny Crosby, the Beguines welcome us to be "filled with his goodness, lost in his love." The final goal of the Christian life is to immerse ourselves in God's bottomless love and grace.

As human beings created in God's image we possess the greatest dignity. Coming from the age of chivalry, the women of this volume describe our souls in terms of "nobility"—there is nothing common about us since we are fashioned in divine likeness. For this reason we can submerge ourselves in God's depths.

Likewise, we have undiscovered depths within us. Hadewijch describes the unsearchable deepness, the true profundity, within each of us: "Now understand the deepest essence of your soul, what 'soul' is. Soul is a being that can be beheld by God and by which, again, God can be beheld. Soul is also a being that wishes to content God. . . . If it maintains this worthy state, the soul is a bottomless abyss in which God suffices to himself. . . . And as long as God does not belong to the soul in his totality, he does not truly satisfy it."[1]

Such deep places can be filled and fulfilled only by the Almighty. We are spiritual beings, so only the fullness of God can satisfy our soul. Yet because God is fathomless, the more we have of him, the more we desire. If we are truly encountering God, we will continually experience fresh craving of him. Hadewijch describes this longing:

> My soul melts away
> In the madness of Love;
> The abyss into which she hurls me
> Is deeper than the sea;
> For Love's new deep abyss
> Renews my wound:
> I look for no more health
> Until I experience Love as all new to me.[2]

UNFATHOMABLE GOD

For the most part modern Christians have lost a sense of awe for God's inscrutability. While contemporary culture often assumes that knowledge of all things, including God, is within our grasp, medieval believers understood that the greatest realities are a mystery beyond our ken. Were we able to comprehend God he would not be worthy of our love or worship.

The God of the Bible is vast, beyond our comprehension and far deeper than our most profound understanding. Hadewijch writes:

All that man comes to in his thought of God, and all that he can understand of him or imagine under any outward form, is not God. For if men could grasp him and conceive of him with their sense images and with their thoughts, God would be less than man, and man's love for him would soon run out.[3]

Believers of the thirteenth century were fascinated with God's greatness, grandeur and impenetrability. They understood that we were created to long for the infinite. As Beatrice of Nazareth states, we desire to be drawn into "the eternity of *minne* [divine love] and the incomprehensibility and the vastness and the inaccessible sublimity and the deep abyss of the Godhead, which is all in all things, and remains incomprehensible in all things, and which is immutable, all-existent, all-capable, all-comprehending, and all-powerfully working."[4]

Scripture gives us glimpses of the divine—quick peeks, as it were—that reveal a shimmer of God's glory but ultimately conceal God's infinite majesty in mystery. When he descended on Mount Sinai, "there was thunder and lightning, with a thick cloud over the mountain. . . . The smoke billowed up from it like smoke from a furnace, the whole mountain trembled violently" (Exodus 19:16-18). When David cried for help, God heard from heaven and came down:

The earth trembled and quaked,
    and the foundations of the mountains shook;
    they trembled because he was angry.

> Smoke rose from his nostrils;
>   consuming fire came from his mouth,
>   burning coals blazed out of it.
> He parted the heavens and came down;
>   dark clouds were under his feet.
> He mounted the cherubim and flew;
>   he soared on the wings of the wind.
> He made darkness his covering, his canopy around him.
>   (Psalm 18:7-11)

In the New Testament we are still called to "worship God acceptably with reverence and awe, for our 'God is a consuming fire'" (Hebrews 12:28-29). Such a God is beyond comprehension. Paul declares that he preaches the "unfathomable riches of Christ" (Ephesians 3:8 NASB). Not only is God deep without measure, his love is expansive beyond our conception. For this reason we need the eyes of our own hearts supernaturally opened in order for us to "grasp how wide and long and high and deep is the love of Christ, and to know this love that surpasses knowledge—that [we] may be filled to the measure of all the fullness of God" (Ephesians 3:18-19). Indeed the only way to "know" that which "surpasses knowledge" is by having our spiritual eyes opened.

Such an inscrutable God is the God the Beguines worshiped. They spoke of him as the unfathomable depths—the abyss. While the term "abyss" often carries a negative connotation today, this is the word used most often by the women of the thirteenth-century renewal to describe God's unsounded depths. He is unsearchable in his being and his wisdom.

God's love can never be fully plumbed. We can spend all eternity exploring God's vastness and never find an end or limit. In a letter Hadewijch prays for a friend: "God be with you and make known to you . . . the unspeakable, vast sweetness of his ardent sweet Nature, which is so deep and so unfathomable that in wondrousness and unknowableness he is deeper and darker than the abyss."[5]

TAKING THE PLUNGE

The image of sinking is a many-faceted metaphor. To submerge ourselves in God is to put our roots deep down into his unplumbed goodness. It is to abandon ourselves into the sea of his immeasurable wisdom and providence. Likewise, to sink down is to humble ourselves and give up control. If we are to experience the Lord's full love for us, we must learn to release our desire to be in control. Hadewijch invites us, "O dear child, lose yourself wholly in him with all your soul! And lose in him likewise whatever befalls you . . . for our adversaries are many, but if we can stand firm, we shall reach our full growth."[6]

When we are in relationship with God Almighty, we cannot be the ones in charge. Much of our contemporary spirituality seeks to place God—and our walk with him—into a neat, orderly box. Such spiritual formation, however, is merely a fantasy of our own making. Vibrant, living relationship does not fit into quick quiet times. Moreover, any "god" contained by our boxes and controlled by our expectations is not the God of Scripture who rides on the winds of the storm and in whose presence the mountains shake to their very foundation.

Sinking can also be a terrifying metaphor. It is reminiscent of drowning in the fathomless ocean. Although it is frightening to abandon ourselves and descend in humility, the Beguines assure us that we will not be lost or destroyed. God's principles are the inverse of worldly ones. To die is to live; to lower ourselves is to be lifted up. Thus Hadewijch asserts that "the deeper sunk in Love, the higher ascended."[7] Mechthild echoes:

But the deeper I sink,
The sweeter I drink.[8]

INTIMATE UNION

In the unfathomable depths the Lord calls us into oneness with himself. While we are united with him in our spiritual birth, this is only the beginning point of our union. Like a good marriage, full oneness with the Divine is realized only over many years of growing together. God's desire is not simply to redeem us but to reconcile us and restore us to full fellowship with himself (2 Corinthians 5:11-21).

Throughout Scripture God woos his people to himself. "I have loved you with an everlasting love," declares the Lord in Jeremiah 31:3. "I have drawn you with loving-kindness." God states in Hosea 2:14, "I am now going to allure her . . . into the desert and speak tenderly to her." Hadewijch recognizes God's wooing in her life, and she responds with tender acceptance to his pursuit:

> God, who created all things
> And who, above all, is particularly Love,
> I supplicate to consent,
>   According to his pleasure,
> That Love now draw the loving soul to herself
>   In the closest union possible to Love.[9]

Using intimate imagery, Mechthild describes one of her deep experiences of union with the Lord. She employs the standard medieval terminology of God's "kiss" to refer to her ecstasy in the Lord's presence. "She stood there, her heart melting, looked upon her Lover and said, 'O Lord, . . . am I now lost in you? I cannot even remember earth or any of my interior sufferings. . . . You have elevated me utterly beyond my worth.'" She continues, "Then she knelt down and thanked him for his favors and, taking her crown from her head, put it on the rose-colored scars on his feet and begged that she might come closer to him. He took her in his divine arms . . . and looked her in the face. Well, was she kissed at all? In the kiss she was drawn up to the most sublime heights."[10]

Thus, Mechthild sings of this intimate union with the Lord that is available to us as believers:

I am in you
And you are in me.
We could not be closer,
For we two have flowed into one
And have been poured into one mold.
Thus shall we remain forever content.[11]

UNION OF WILLS

Contemporary Christians will benefit from wise spiritual guides with regard to our oneness with God, especially in light of the pantheistic merger of the human and divine that various Buddhist and New Age teachers proffer today. In reaction to their concept of an impersonal dissipation into nirvana, many believers renounce any notion of spiritual union. Yet such wholesale rejection of the topic fails to recognize the New Testament's promise of an appropriate oneness with God.

Jesus commands us to abide in him, and he promises to abide in us (John 15:4-7). In John 17:21 Jesus prays "that they may all be one; even as you, Father, are in Me and I in You, that they also may be in Us" (NASB). Thus our Lord prays that, as well as being one with each other, we would be one with him and the Father just as he and the Father are one. That is quite one! Yet as the Father and the Son remain distinct persons in the midst of their intimate union, we as believers remain distinct persons even in our deepest oneness with God.

Biblical oneness is not a cosmic merger of the divine and human but rather the oneness of personhood—the same oneness that the persons of the Trinity share. Although we experience the deepest possible union with the triune God, we forever remain created beings while God remains the uncreated Creator. This is the inti-

mate joining together of persons—human and divine. Paul summarizes such unity in 1 Corinthians 6:17: "He who unites himself
with the Lord is one with him in spirit."

In contrast to the notion of losing our uniqueness as a person
or being absorbed into God, Christian theologians through the
centuries have described union with the Lord in terms of being
united in will. Such union of wills is what the Beguines long for in
their absolute obedience to Christ. "To live sincerely according to
the will of Love," writes Hadewijch, "is to be so perfectly one in
the will of veritable Love, in order to content her, that—even if
one had another wish—one would choose or wish nothing except
to desire above all what Love wills."[12]

For Mechthild that most profound union of our will with the
Lord takes place as we are caught up in the sheer elation of the
Lord's presence. When our soul begins to experience the ecstasy
of God's love, the soul becomes united with God "in such a way
that whatever he wills she wills as well, and they can be united in
complete union no other way."[13]

Hadewijch prays that we would experience such union in our
relationship with God: "And may he also make known to you, in
truth and reality, that sweet and delightful union the experience
of which he still gives to his dear friends who conform to his holy
sweet love above all things."[14] As we give up our will and take on
the yoke of God's will in our lives, we are united in a deep way
with the Lord. "Thus," says Hadewijch, "shall there be a single
meeting in the one will of unitive love."[15] In poetic fashion she
expands on this theme:

> What is this light burden of Love
> And this sweet-tasting yoke?
> It is the noble load of the spirit,
> With which Love touches the loving soul
> And unites it to her with one will

And with one being, without reversal. . . .

To those who give themselves thus to content Love,
What great wonders shall happen!
With love they shall cleave in oneness to Love.[16]

FINAL CONSUMMATION IN HEAVEN

So long as we are on earth, our experience of union with the Lord will always be limited and incomplete. Full union with the Lord comes only in heaven, the promised wedding feast, when the bride is finally and fully united to the beloved Bridegroom. This is the eternal hope of all believers and blessed anticipation of all the medieval women who set themselves apart as brides of Christ. Hadewijch declares that she is firm in confidence that "Love one day will embrace me in oneness."[17]

Mechthild also expresses her longing for that eternal union with God in heaven. "Here the soul presented herself in . . . eternal love to God and in restless longing to go to God. Thus does she speak: 'The long waiting is coming to an end. In the future God and the soul shall be united, unseparated forever.'"[18]

Although we must persevere through the difficult times in this life, we refuse to succumb to discouragement and look forward to an intimate union with God in eternity. Our spiritual marriage with the Bridegroom will one day be consummated in heaven. Mechthild looks forward to that day and prays for herself, the Beguines and, by extension, all who have set themselves apart for Christ.

Receive, Lord, your brides, and approach them with the lilies of pure chastity all their days.

Receive, Lord, your brides, and approach them with the roses of diligent work for a good end.

Receive, Lord, your brides, and approach them with the violets of profound humility and lead them to your bridal bed and, united inseparably with them, embrace them with all love forever. Amen.[19]

Thus we come to an end of the story of the Beguines—women of God who submerged their lives in the pursuit of one thing. By their example and through their writing, these devout women continue to welcome all believers into God's depths and the most intimate union possible with Christ. Through their brilliant images, they bid us come. That invitation is accompanied with a promise: that one day we too will be embraced forever by God in love!

Personal Response
Drinking from Springs of Living Water

Reflection and Journaling

How does contemplating creation give you a fresh perspective of divine majesty and power? Reflect on Job 38–41 to gain a fresh portrait of God's grandeur. How have you been like Job and his friends who assumed they had God figured out?

What would sinking down into God's unfathomable depths entail for your life? What would you need to let go of? What scares you about submerging yourself in God?

Scripture

Read Jesus' parable of the ten virgins and the wedding feast in Matthew 25:1-13. How do you identify with the five foolish virgins or the five wise ones? What image do you have of the great wedding feast?

Read Revelation 21:1-7. In what ways do you long for the consummation of time when God wipes away tear from your eye and makes all things new? How does that image give you hope in the present?

Creativity and Action

Paul prays that we would be able "to grasp how wide and long and high and deep is the love of Christ" (Ephesians 3:18). What does that look like to you? Can you express it—at least in part—through song, in a poem, via dance or by creating a work of art?

Community

Share your creative expression of Ephesians 3:18 with a spiritual friend, your family or your small group. How has creative expression helped you better to "grasp how wide and long and high and deep" God's love is? How has sharing with them enabled both you and them to grasp divine love in a fuller way?

With a friend or in a small group, read aloud or sing the hymn "Blessed Assurance." Turn the words "filled with his goodness, lost in his love" into a prayer. Perhaps each one wants to write out his or her prayer, then share them with one another. Finally, take time as a group to pray out loud your hearts' longing to be lost in God's love.

Acknowledgments

As THE BEGUINES MODEL for us the centrality of Christian community, I want to honor those whose lives, prayer and fellowship have enabled me to write this book.

First, thank you to my wife, Sharon, for introducing me to the Beguines' writings and for exploring Belgium with me as we visited numerous beguinages that still stand today. Thank you for your constant encouragement and support in my writing this book.

Special thanks to my parents, Earl and Bea Myers, for their reading various sections of my work and providing continual love and inspiration over the years.

Thank you to Carol Schulz and Lois Paine for valuable input on my manuscript and constant prayer support. Thank you to the many friends who have reviewed chapters of this work and given helpful suggestions, as well as students who have read parts of this material and provided useful feedback.

I am especially grateful to my editor, Dave Zimmerman, for providing critical input as well as cheering me on in the process. As well, the editorial staff at InterVarsity Press has been tremendously helpful along the way. I also want to express appreciation to the administration and trustees of Crown College for granting me a sabbatical as I finished my book.

Notes

Introduction

[1]Mechthild of Magdeburg, *The Flowing Light of the Godhead*, trans. Frank Tobin, The Classics of Western Spirituality (Mahwah, N.J.: Paulist, 1998), p. 213.

[2]Hadewijch, *Hadewijch: The Complete Works*, trans. Mother Columba Hart, The Classics of Western Spirituality (Mahwah, N.J.: Paulist, 1980), p. 56.

Chapter 1: The Beguines

[1]For a very readable introduction to the early Beguine movement in Belgium, see Walter Simons, *Cities of Ladies: Beguine Communities in the Medieval Low Countries, 1200-1565* (Philadelphia: University of Pennsylvania Press, 2001).

[2]More than three hundred years before Martin Luther, there was no division between Roman Catholic and Protestant as we have known since the 1500s. In the Middle Ages everyone was part of the one Catholic Church. During this time waves of revival brought the gospel to untold numbers in Europe, leading them into a personal faith in Christ.

[3]As quoted in Simons, *Cities of Ladies*, p. 35.

[4]Walter Simons makes a convincing argument for the derivation of *Beguine* from the term *bèguer*, in *Cities of Ladies*, pp. 121-23. Another theory is that *Beguine* is related to the word *beige*, since their simple dresses were made from beige cloth. Herbert Grundmann maintains that the term *Beguine*

derived from *Albigensians,* in *Religious Movements of the Middle Ages,* trans. Steven Rowan (Notre Dame, Ind.: University of Notre Dame Press, 1995), p. 80.

[5]The Beguines were among various groups from the twelfth to the fifteenth century who sought such middle ground between monasticism and active life in the world. A very readable summary of these vast evangelical movements can be found in R. W. Southern, *Western Society and the Church in the Middle Ages,* Penguin History of the Church (London: Penguin, 1970): 2, as well as C. H. Lawrence, *Medieval Monasticism: Forms of Religious Life in Western Europe in the Middle Ages,* 3rd ed. (Harlow, U.K.: Pearson Education, 2001). For an in-depth description of these renewal movements and their relationship with the Beguines, see Grundmann, *Religious Movements,* and Ernest W. McDonnell, *The Beguines and Beghards in Medieval Culture, with Special Emphasis on the Belgian Scene* (New Brunswick, N.J.: Rutgers University Press, 1954).

[6]Mechthild of Magdeburg, *The Flowing Light of the Godhead,* trans. Frank Tobin, The Classics of Western Spirituality (Mahwah, N.J.: Paulist, 1998), p. 53.

[7]By the time of the Beguine movement a priest from Liège named Lambert le Bègue had the book of Acts translated into Dutch, as well as a number of devotional biographies of women's lives. In German territories, so many translations of the Bible were being made that by Martin Luther's time in the early 1500s, eighteen versions were available in German. See William R. Estep, *Renaissance and Reformation* (Grand Rapids: Eerdmans, 1986), p. 135. What made Luther's translation so valuable was his style, which helped standardize the German language, and the fact that he based his translation on the Greek and Hebrew texts rather than the Vulgate.

[8]Hadewijch, *Hadewijch: The Complete Works,* trans. Mother Columba Hart, The Classics of Western Spirituality (Mahwah, N.J.: Paulist, 1980), p. 77.

[9]As quoted in McDonnell, *Beguines and Beghards,* p. 148.

[10]Simons, *Cities of Ladies,* p. 81.

[11]Rik Uytterhoeven, *The Groot Begijnhof of Leuven,* trans. Guido Latré (Leuven, Belgium: Leuven University Press, 2000), p. 11.

[12]Countess Johanna founded beguinages in Ghent, Courtrai, Bruges, Ypres, Douai, Lille, Valenciennes, Mons and several other locations. See McDonnell, *Beguines and Beghards,* pp. 205-17. In his appendixes, Simons also documents the rapid development of beguinages across Belgium.

[13]McDonnell, *Beguines and Beghards,* pp. 218-23.

[14]Simons, *Cities of Ladies,* pp. 51, 54-55, 58, 59.

[15]Protestant and Catholic scholars alike refer to the waves of revival in the

Middle Ages as an "evangelical renewal."

[16]Grundmann, *Religious Movements*, pp. 78, 234.

[17]As quoted in McDonnell, *Beguines and Beghards*, p. 102.

[18]See Bernard of Clairvaux, "Conversion," in *Bernard of Clairvaux: Selected Works*, ed. and trans. G. R. Evans, The Classics of Western Spirituality (Mahwah, N.J.: Paulist, 1987).

[19]For a thorough discussion of the Brethren of the Free Spirit, their theology and their relationship with the Beguines, see Robert E. Lerner, *The Heresy of the Free Spirit in the Later Middle Ages* (Berkeley: University of California Press, 1972). The Beghards—the male counterpart to the Beguines—were especially linked to this heresy. In her book *The Mirror of Simple, Annihilated Souls*, Beguine Margaret Porete leaned in the direction of this teaching. For this reason I have not included her in this overview of the Beguines. Margaret persisted with distributing her book and public preaching of her ideas, which led to her being burned at the stake in 1310. See *Marguerite Porete: The Mirror of Simple Souls*, trans. Ellen L. Babinsky, The Classics of Western Spirituality (Mahwah, N.J.: Paulist, 1993).

[20]Hadewijch, *Complete Works*, pp. 138-39.

Chapter 2: Radical Faith

[1]James of Vitry, *The Life of Mary of Oignies*, in *Two Lives of Marie d'Oignies*, trans. Margot King (Toronto: Peregrina, 2002), p. 86.

[2]Ibid., p. 95.

[3]Ibid., p. 90.

[4]We are told that John approved of Mary's withdrawal to Oignies. However, because the *Vita* centers on Mary, we are told little else about John from this point.

[5]James of Vitry, *Two Lives*, p. 83.

[6]Ibid., p. 53.

[7]Ibid., p. 83.

Chapter 3: Desiring God's Presence

[1]Hadewijch, *Hadewijch: The Complete Works*, trans. Mother Columba Hart, The Classics of Western Spirituality (Mahwah, N.J.: Paulist, 1980), pp. 73-74.

[2]Mechthild of Magdeburg, *The Flowing Light of the Godhead*, trans. Frank Tobin, The Classics of Western Spirituality (Mahwah, N.J.: Paulist, 1998), p. 287.

[3]Ibid., pp. 41-42.

[4]James of Vitry, "The Life of Mary of Oignies," in *Two Lives of Marie d'Oignies*,

trans. Margot King (Toronto: Peregrina, 2002), p. 80.

[5]Hadewijch, *Complete Works*, p. 352.

[6]Ibid., p. 86.

[7]As quoted in Ernst McDonnell, *The Beguines and Beghards in Medieval Culture, with Special Emphasis on the Belgian Scene* (New Brunswick, N.J.: Rutgers University Press, 1954), p. 148.

[8]Pedro Arrupe as quoted in Richard Rohr, *Everything Belongs: The Gift of Contemplative Prayer* (New York: Crossroad, 2003), p. 122.

[9]Hadewijch, *Complete Works*, p. 168. See similar passages on pp. 50, 133, 150 and 173.

[10]Ruth Haley Barton, *Sacred Rhythms: Arranging Our Lives for Spiritual Transformation* (Downers Grove, Ill.: InterVarsity Press, 2006), p. 50.

[11]M. Robert Mulholland, *Shaped by the Word: The Power of Scripture in Spiritual Formation*, 2nd ed. (Nashville: Upper Room, 2005), p. 95.

[12]Henri Nouwen, *Making All Things New: An Invitation to the Spiritual Life* (San Francisco: HarperSanFrancisco, 1981), p. 69.

Chapter 4: Seasons of the Soul

[1]Her spiritual biography is available in English as *The Life of Beatrice of Nazareth, 1200-1268*, trans. Roger DeGanck (Kalamazoo, Mich.: Cistercian, 1991).

[2]Beatrice expands on Richard of St. Victor's *Four Manners of Violent Love*, presenting a more dynamic model than Richard's and offering insight from her feminine point of view.

[3]Bernard McGinn, *The Flowering of Mysticism: Men and Women in the New Mysticism—1200-1350*, The Presence of God: A History of Western Christian Mysticism (New York: Crossroad, 1998, 2005), 3:166.

[4]*Life of Beatrice of Nazareth*, p. 291.

[5]Ibid.

[6]Ibid., p. 293.

[7]Ibid., p. 295.

[8]Ibid., pp. 295-97.

[9]Ibid., p. 299.

[10]Ibid., p. 301.

[11]Ibid.

[12]Ibid., p. 303.

[13]Ibid., p. 305.

[14]Ibid.

[15]Ibid., p. 311.

[16]Ibid., pp. 313-15.

[17]Ibid., p. 319
[18]Ibid., p. 317.
[19]Ibid., p. 315.
[20]McGinn, *Flowering of Mysticism*, p. 173.
[21]Howard R. Macy, *Rhythms of the Inner Life: Yearning for Closeness with God* (Colorado Springs: Chariot Victor, 1988).

Chapter 5: Creative Community

[1]As quoted in Walter Simons, *Cities of Ladies: Beguine Communities in the Medieval Low Countries, 1200-1565* (Philadelphia: University of Pennsylvania Press, 2001), p. 82.

[2]See Ernest W. McDonnell, *The Beguines and Beghards in Medieval Culture, with Special Emphasis on the Belgian Scene* (New Brunswick, N.J.: Rutgers University Press, 1954), pp. 246-65.

[3]Shane Claiborne, *The Irresistible Revolution: Living as an Ordinary Radical* (Grand Rapids: Zondervan, 2006), p. 296.

[4]Aelred of Rievaulx, *Spiritual Friendship*, trans. Mary Eugenia Laker (Kalamazoo, Mich.: Cistercian, 1977). Aelred was a friend of Bernard of Clairvaux's and an abbot in the Cistercian movement that had such an impact on the Beguines and other spiritual renewal groups of the time.

[5]See *Johannes Tauler: Sermons*, trans. Maria Shrady, The Classics of Western Spirituality (Mahwah, N.J.: Paulist, 1985).

[6]Dietrich Bonhoeffer, *Life Together*, trans. John W. Doberstein (San Francisco: HarperSanFrancisco, 1954), p. 27.

[7]Ibid., p. 77.

[8]James M. Houston, *The Prayer: Deepening Your Friendship with God*, Soul's Longing Series (Colorado Springs: Cook Communications Ministries, 2007), 3:53-54. Houston's book was originally titled *The Transforming Friendship*, because it explores the transforming power of genuine Christian friendship as well as that of intimate relationship with God in prayer.

Chapter 6: Savoring Inner Sweetness

[1]Bernard McGinn states, "Receiving Communion (which they apparently did quite frequently, often more than once a week) was the source of their vivid experiences of the heavenly world and especially of their union with Jesus, the Divine Bridegroom." *The Flowering of Mysticism: Men and Women in the New Mysticism—1200-1350*, The Presence of God: A History of Western Christian Mysticism (New York: Crossroad, 1998, 2005), 3:270.

[2]Hadewijch, *Hadewijch: The Complete Works*, trans. Mother Columba Hart, The Classics of Western Spirituality (Mahwah, N.J.: Paulist, 1980), p. 112.

[3]Ibid., p. 161.

[4]Ibid., p. 88.

[5]Ibid., pp. 66-67.

[6]Ibid., p. 67. Hart notes that, in this letter, Hadewijch is paraphrasing thoughts on spiritual sweetness set forth by Richard of St. Victor in his *Commentary on the Song of Songs.*

[7]Ibid., p. 164.

[8]Ibid., p. 67.

[9]Ibid., p. 54.

[10]Ibid.

[11]Ibid., pp. 119-20.

[12]Ibid., p. 75. Here Hadewijch echoes Beatrice of Nazareth's third mode of holy love.

[13]Ibid., p. 48.

[14]See A. W. Tozer, *The Pursuit of God* (Camp Hill, Penn.: Christian Publications, 1993).

[15]For a thorough discussion of various addictions and how they work in our lives, see Gerald G. May, *Addiction and Grace* (San Francisco: Harper & Row, 1988).

[16]One of the best explorations of the benefits and dangers of spiritual experiences is Jonathan Edwards, *Religious Affections: A Christian's Character Before God,* ed. James M. Houston, Classics of Faith and Devotion (Vancouver, B.C.: Regent College Publishing, 2003).

[17]Hadewijch, *Complete Works,* p. 60.

Chapter 7: Valiant Knights and Untamed Wilderness

[1]Hadewijch, *Hadewijch: The Complete Works,* trans. Mother Columba Hart, The Classics of Western Spirituality (Mahwah, N.J.: Paulist, 1980), p. 149. Unfortunately, because Hadewijch's poems are translated into English, they lose their rhyme and some of their beauty. Nevertheless, their message is still powerful.

[2]Ibid., p. 171.

[3]Ibid., p. 224.

[4]Ibid., p. 136.

[5]Ibid., p. 49.

[6]Ibid., p. 234. It should be noted that Hadewijch did not title any of her poems. The titles provided here are the ones supplied by her translator.

[7]Ibid., p. 231.

[8]Ibid., p. 218.

[9]Ibid., p. 183.

[10]Ibid., p. 239.

[11]Ibid., p. 73.

[12]Ibid., p. 252.

[13]Ibid., p. 147.

[14]Ibid., p. 168.

[15]Ibid., pp. 224-25.

[16]Ibid., p. 151.

[17]M. Robert. Mulholland, *Invitation to a Journey: A Roadmap for Spiritual Formation* (Downers Grove, Ill.: InterVarsity Press, 1993), p. 37.

[18]Brennan Manning, *Abba's Child: The Cry of the Heart for Intimate Belonging* (Colorado Springs: NavPress, 2002), pp. 34-36.

[19]Robert M. Mulholland, *The Deeper Journey: The Spirituality of Discovering Your True Self* (Downers Grove, Ill.: InterVarsity Press, 2006).

[20]Ibid., p. 47.

[21]Ibid., p. 49.

[22]James M. Houston, *The Desire: Satisfying the Heart,* Soul's Longing Series (Colorado Springs: Victor, 2007), 1:209.

[23]Ibid.

Chapter 8: Flowing In and Out of God's Presence

[1]Mechthild of Magdeburg, *The Flowing Light of the Godhead,* trans. Frank Tobin, The Classics of Western Spirituality (Mahwah, N.J.: Paulist, 1998), pp. 139-40.

[2]Mechthild wrote in Middle Low German. Although no copies of her work exist in the original language, we have translations of *Flowing Light of the Godhead* in Middle High German.

[3]While the title of the Paulist volume includes the direct article "the," that article is not present in German. The paradigm of flowing out and back comes from Christian Neoplatonic writers, especially the works of Pseudo-Dionysius. Joining Mechthild and Hadewijch in their use of such imagery are Meister Eckhart, Johannes Tauler, Jan van Ruysbroeck and others of the thirteenth and fourteenth centuries. The writings of William of St. Thierry—circulated under the name of his friend, Bernard of Clairvaux—helped to popularize this paradigm of the Father's flowing forth in the procession of the Son and Spirit, and their return in perfect love for each other. William also emphasized the participation of believers in this trinitarian love.

[4]Mechthild, *Flowing Light,* p. 50.

[5]Ibid., p. 314.

[6]Ibid., p. 48.

[7]Ibid., p. 226.

[8]Ibid., pp. 323-24.

[9]Ibid., p. 164.

[10]Ibid., p. 324.

[11]Ibid., p. 195.

[12]Ibid., p. 187.

[13]Ibid., p. 196.

[14]Ibid., p. 256.

[15]Ibid., pp. 223-24.

[16]Ibid., p. 224.

[17]Ibid., p. 301.

[18]Ibid.

[19]Ibid., p. 207.

[20]Ibid., p. 238.

[21]James M. Houston, *The Prayer: Deepening Your Friendship with God*, Soul's Longing Series (Colorado Springs: Victor, 2007), 3:55.

[22]Margaret Guenther, *Holy Listening: The Art of Spiritual Direction* (Boston: Cowley, 1992), p. 13.

[23]Richard J. Foster and James Bryan Smith, *Devotional Classics: Selected Readings for Individuals and Groups* (San Francisco: HarperSanFrancisco, 1990), p. 99.

[24]Wayne Oates, *Nurturing Silence in a Noisy Heart* (Minneapolis: Augsburg Fortress, 1996), p. 38.

[25]Thomas R. Kelly, *A Testament of Devotion* (San Francisco: HarperSanFrancisco, 1992), pp. 8-10.

[26]Ibid.

[27]Mechthild, *Flowing Light*, pp. 239-40.

Chapter 9: Intimacy with the Lord

[1]Augustinian canons were secular priests who lived in community much like monks. However, they followed what is referred as St. Augustine's Rule rather than Benedict's Rule, allowing them more free time for ministry or study. See C. H. Lawrence, *Medieval Monasticism: Forms of Religious Life in Western Europe in the Middle Ages*, 3rd ed. (Harlow, U.K.: Pearson Education, 2001), pp. 160-68.

[2]Mechthild of Magdeburg, *The Flowing Light of the Godhead*, trans. Frank Tobin, The Classics of Western Spirituality (Mahwah, N.J.: Paulist, 1998), p. 274.

[3]Ibid., p. 44.

[4]Ibid., p. 283.

[5]Ibid., p. 44.
[6]Ibid., p. 52.
[7]Ibid., pp. 40-41.
[8]Ibid., pp. 88-89.
[9]Ibid., p. 327.
[10]Ibid., p. 95
[11]Ibid.

Chapter 10: Transformation Through Trials

[1]Mechthild of Magdeburg, The Flowing Light of the Godhead, trans. Frank Tobin, The Classics of Western Spirituality (Mahwah, N.J.: Paulist, 1998), p. 334.
[2]Ibid., p. 333.
[3]Ibid., p. 54.
[4]Ibid., p. 322.
[5]Ibid., pp. 117-18.
[6]Ibid., p. 303.
[7]Ibid., p. 301.
[8]Ibid., p. 249.
[9]Ibid., p. 231.
[10]Ibid., p. 240.
[11]Ibid., p. 180.
[12]Ibid., p. 194.
[13]Ibid., p. 52.
[14]Ibid., p. 302.
[15]Ibid., p. 206.
[16]Ibid., p. 325.
[17]Ibid., p. 277.
[18]Ibid., p. 149.
[19]Ibid., p. 225.
[20]Ibid., p. 299.

Chapter 11: Beautiful Life of Freedom

[1]Andrew Murray, Absolute Surrender (Springdale, Penn.: Whitaker House, 1981), p. 28.
[2]A. W. Tozer, The Pursuit of God (Camp Hill, Penn.: Christian Publications, 1993), p. 43.
[3]Dietrich Bonhoeffer, The Cost of Discipleship (New York: Touchstone, 1995), p. 11.
[4]Tozer, Pursuit of God, pp. 43-44.

[5]Ibid., p. 45.

[6]Mechthild of Magdeburg, *The Flowing Light of the Godhead*, trans. Frank Tobin, The Classics of Western Spirituality (Mahwah, N.J.: Paulist, 1998), p. 96.

[7]Hadewijch, *Hadewijch: The Complete Works*, trans. Mother Columba Hart, The Classics of Western Spirituality (Mahwah, N.J.: Paulist, 1980), p. 114. Although Hadewijch often used the terms "wandering" and "prison" in a figurative sense, most commentators believe that these references are to literal eviction and homelessness.

[8]Ibid., p. 56.

[9]Ibid., pp. 321-22.

[10]Mechthild, *Flowing Light,* p. 303.

[11]Hadewijch, *Complete Works*, p. 339.

[12]Mechthild, *Flowing Light*, 266.

[13]Ibid., p. 287.

[14]Ibid., p. 153.

[15]Hadewijch, *Complete Works*, p. 63.

[16]Mechthild, *Flowing Light*, p. 69.

[17]This caution in choosing spiritual disciplines is highlighted by Francis de Sales, *Introduction to the Devout Life* (New York: Vintage, 2002), pp. 85-88.

[18]Mechthild, *Flowing Light*, p. 53.

[19]Hadewijch, *Complete Works*, p. 247.

[20]Ibid., p. 90.

Chapter 12: Lost in God's Love

[1]Hadewijch, *Hadewijch: The Complete Works*, trans. Mother Columba Hart, The Classics of Western Spirituality (Mahwah, N.J.: Paulist, 1980), p. 86.

[2]Ibid., p. 145.

[3]Ibid., p. 70.

[4]Bernard McGinn, *The Flowering of Mysticism: Men and Women in the New Mysticism—1200-1350,* The Presence of God: A History of Western Christian Mysticism (New York: Crossroad, 1998, 2005), 3:173.

[5]Hadewijch, *Complete Works*, p. 107.

[6]Ibid., p. 55.

[7]Ibid., p. 204.

[8]Mechthild of Magdeburg, *The Flowing Light of the Godhead*, trans. Frank Tobin, The Classics of Western Spirituality (Mahwah, N.J.: Paulist, 1998), p. 156.

[9]Hadewijch, *Complete Works*, p. 181.

[10]Mechthild, *Flowing Light*, p. 102.

[11]Ibid., p. 111.

[12]Hadewijch, *Complete Works*, p. 58.
[13]Mechthild, *Flowing Light*, p. 226.
[14]Hadewijch, *Complete Works*, p. 76.
[15]Ibid., p. 75.
[16]Ibid., pp. 158-59.
[17]Ibid., p. 178.
[18]Mechthild, *Flowing Light*, p. 315.
[19]Ibid., p. 300.

Suggestions for Further Reading

Chapter 1: The Beguines

Foster, Richard, and Gayle Beebe. *Longing for God: Seven Paths of Christian Devotion.* Downers Grove, Ill.: InterVarsity Press, 2005.

Grundmann, Herbert. *Religious Movements of the Middle Ages.* Translated by Steven Rowan. Notre Dame, Ind.: University of Notre Dame Press, 1995.

Lawrence, C. H. *Medieval Monasticism: Forms of Religious Life in Western Europe in the Middle Ages.* 3rd ed. Harlow, U.K.: Pearson Education, 2001.

Leclercq, Jean, Francois Vandenbroucke and Louis Bouyer. *The Spirituality of the Middle Ages.* A History of Christian Spirituality 2. New York: Seabury, 1968.

Lerner, Robert E. *The Heresy of the Free Spirit in the Later Middle Ages.* Berkeley: University of California Press, 1972.

McDonnell, Ernest W. *The Beguines and Beghards in Medieval Culture, with Special Emphasis on the Belgian Scene.* New Brunswick, N.J.: Rutgers University Press, 1954.

McGinn, Bernard. *The Flowering of Mysticism: Men and Women in the New Mysticism—1200-1350.* The Presence of God: A History of Western Christian Mysticism 3. New York: Crossroad, 1998, 2005.

Simons, Walter. *Cities of Ladies: Beguine Communities in the Medieval Low Countries, 1200-1565.* Philadelphia: University of Pennsylvania Press, 2001.

Sittser, Gerald. *Water from a Deep Well: Christian Spirituality from Early Martyrs to Modern Missionaries.* Downers Grove, Ill.: InterVarsity Press, 2007.

Southern, R. W. *Western Society and the Church in the Middle Ages.* Pelican History of the Church 2. London: Penguin, 1970.

Chapter 2: Radical Faith

Bessenecker, Scott. *The New Friars: The Emerging Movement Serving the World's Poor.* Downers Grove, Ill.: InterVarsity Press, 2006.

Campolo, Tony, and Mary Albert Darling. *The God of Intimacy and Action: Reconnecting Ancient Spiritual Practices, Evangelism, and Justice.* San Francisco: Jossey-Bass, 2007.

James of Vitry. "The Life of Mary of Oignies." In *Two Lives of Marie d'Oignies.* Translated by Margot King. Toronto, Ontario: Peregrina, 2002.

McManus, Erwin R. *Chasing Daylight: Dare to Live a Life of Adventure.* Nashville: Thomas Nelson, 2002.

Piper, John. *Desiring God: Meditations of a Christian Hedonist.* Sisters, Ore.: Multnomah, 1996.

Chapter 3: Desiring God's Presence

Barton, Ruth Haley. *Sacred Rhythms: Arranging Our Lives for Spiritual Transformation.* Downers Grove, Ill.: InterVarsity Press, 2006.

Doherty, Catherine. *Poustinia: Encountering God in Silence, Solitude and Prayer.* Combermere, Ont.: Madonna House, 2000.

Foster, Richard J. *Prayer: Finding the Heart's True Home.* San Francisco: HarperSanFrancisco, 1992.

———. *Streams of Living Water: Celebrating the Great Traditions of Christian Faith.* San Francisco: HarperSanFrancisco, 1998.

Hall, Thelma. *Too Deep for Words: Rediscovering Lectio Divina.* Mahwah, N.J.: Paulist, 1988.

Mulholland, M. Robert. *Shaped by the Word: The Power of Scripture in Spiritual Formation.* 2nd ed. Nashville: Upper Room, 2005.

Nouwen, Henri. *Making All Things New: An Invitation to the Spiritual Life.* San Francisco: HarperSanFrancisco, 1981.

Chapter 4: Seasons of the Soul

Augustine of Hippo. *Confessions.* Translated by Henry Chadwick. Oxford: Oxford University Press, 1991.

Bunyan, John. *The Pilgrim's Progress: From This World to That Which Is to Come.* Uhrichsville, Ohio: Barbour, 1993.

Fowler, James W. *Stages of Faith: The Psychology of Human Development and the Quest for Meaning.* San Francisco: HarperSanFrancisco, 1995.

The Life of Beatrice of Nazareth, 1200-1268. Translated by Roger DeGanck. Kalamazoo, Mich.: Cistercian, 1991.

Macy, Howard R. *Rhythms of the Inner Life: Yearning for Closeness with God.* Colorado Springs: Chariot Victor, 1988.

Mulholland, M. Robert. *Invitation to a Journey: A Road Map for Spiritual Formation.* Downers Grove, Ill.: InterVarsity Press, 1993.

Chapter 5: Creative Community

Aelred of Rievaulx. *Spiritual Friendship.* Translated by Mary Eugenia Laker. Kalamazoo, Mich.: Cistercian, 1977.

Bakke, Jeannette A. *Holy Invitations: Exploring Spiritual Direction.* Grand Rapids: Baker, 2000.

Benner, David G. *Sacred Companions: The Gift of Spiritual Friendship and Direction.* Downers Grove, Ill.: InterVarsity Press, 2002.

Bonhoeffer, Dietrich. *Life Together.* Translated by John W. Doberstein. San Francisco: HarperSanFrancisco, 1954.

Guenther, Margaret. *Holy Listening: The Art of Spiritual Direction.* Boston: Crowley, 1992.

Houston, James M. *The Prayer: Deepening Your Friendship with God.* Soul's Longing Series 3. Colorado Springs: Victor, 2007.

Chapter 6: Savoring Inner Sweetness

Edwards, Jonathan. *Religious Affections: A Christian's Character Before God.* Edited by James M. Houston. Classics of Faith and Devotion. Vancouver, B.C.: Regent College Publishing, 2003.

Hadewijch. *Hadewijch: The Complete Works.* Translated by Mother Columba Hart. The Classics of Western Spirituality. Mahwah, N.J.: Paulist, 1980.

Hurnard, Hannah. *Hinds' Feet on High Places: The Original and Complete Allegory with a Devotional for Women by Darien Cooper.* Shippensburg, Penn.: Destiny Image, 2005.

McManus, Erwin R. *Soul Cravings.* Nashville: Thomas Nelson, 2006.

May, Gerald G. *Addiction and Grace.* San Francisco: Harper & Row, 1988.

Chapter 7: Valiant Knights and Untamed Wilderness

Cowman, L. B. *Streams in the Desert.* Edited by James Reimann. Grand Rapids: Zondervan, 1997.

Haase, Albert. *Coming Home to Your True Self: Leaving the Emptiness of False Attractions.* Downers Grove, Ill.: InterVarsity Press, 2008.

Hougen, Judith. *Transformed into Fire: An Invitation to Life in the True Self.* Grand Rapids: Kregel, 2002.

Houston, James M. *The Desire: Satisfying the Heart.* Soul's Longing Series 1. Colorado Springs: Victor, 2007.

John of the Cross. *Dark Night of the Soul.* Translated by E. Allison Peers. Mineola, N.Y.: Dover, 2003.

Manning, Brennan. *Abba's Child: The Cry of the Heart for Intimate Belonging.* Colorado Springs: NavPress, 1994.

Mulholland, M. Robert. *The Deeper Journey: The Spirituality of Discovering Your True Self.* Downers Grove, Ill.: InterVarsity Press, 2006.

Thrall, Bill, Bruce McNicol and John Lynch. *TrueFaced: Trust God and Others with Who You Really Are.* Colorado Springs: NavPress, 2003.

Chapter 8: Flowing In and Out of God's Presence

Barton, Ruth Haley. *Invitation to Solitude and Silence: Experiencing God's Transforming Presence.* Downers Grove, Ill.: InterVarsity Press, 2004.

Foster, Richard J., and James Bryan Smith, eds. *Devotional Classics: Selected Readings for Individuals and Groups.* San Francisco: HarperSanFrancisco, 1990.

Issler, Klaus. *Wasting Time with God: A Christian Spirituality of Friendship with God.* Downers Grove, Ill.: InterVarsity Press, 2001.

Kelly, Thomas. *A Testament of Devotion.* San Francisco: HarperSanFrancisco, 1992.

Mechthild of Magdeburg. *The Flowing Light of the Godhead.* Translated by Frank Tobin. The Classics of Western Spirituality. Mahwah, N.J.: Paulist, 1998.

Oats, Wayne E. *Nurturing Silence in a Noisy Heart: How to Find Inner Peace.* Minneapolis: Augsburg Fortress, 1996.

Palmer, Parker. *The Active Life: A Spirituality of Work, Creativity, and Caring.* New York: HarperCollins, 1990.

Rubietta, Jane. *Resting Place: A Personal Guide to Spiritual Retreats.* Downers Grove, Ill.: InterVarsity Press, 2005.

Chapter 9: Intimacy with the Lord

Bevere, John. *Drawing Near: A Life of Intimacy with God.* Nashville: Thomas Nelson, 2004.

Bowie, Fiona, ed. *Beguine Spirituality: Mystical Writings of Mechthild of Magdeburg, Beatrice of Nazareth, and Hadewijch of Brabant.* Spiritual Classics. New York: Crossroad, 1990.

Gire, Ken. *The Divine Embrace: An Invitation to the Dance of Intimacy with Christ.* Wheaton, Ill.: Tyndale House, 2001.

Humphrey, Edith. *Ecstasy and Intimacy: When the Holy Spirit Meets the Human Spirit.* Grand Rapids: Eerdmans, 2006.

Murk-Jansen, Saskia. *Brides in the Desert: The Spirituality of the Beguines.* Traditions of Spirituality Series. Maryknoll, N.Y.: Orbis, 2004.

Smith, Alice. *Spiritual Intimacy with God: Moving Joyfully into the Deeper Life.* Minneapolis: Bethany House, 2008.

Chapter 10: Transformation Through Trials

Crabb, Larry. *Shattered Dreams: God's Unexpected Pathway to Joy.* Colorado Springs: WaterBrook Press, 2001.

Heuertz, Christopher. *Simple Spirituality: Learning to See God in a Broken World.* Downers Grove, Ill.: InterVarsity Press, 2008.

Miller, Paul. *A Praying Life: Connecting with God in a Distracting World.* Colorado Springs: NavPress, 2009.

Thomas à Kempis. *The Imitation of Christ.* Revised edition. Translated by Joseph N. Tylenda. Vintage Spiritual Classics. New York: Random House, 1998.

Sittser, Gerald. *A Grace Disguised: How the Soul Grows Through Loss.* Grand Rapids: Zondervan, 1995.

Chapter 11: Beautiful Life of Freedom

Bonhoeffer, Dietrich. *The Cost of Discipleship.* New York: Touchstone, 1995.

Caussade, Jean-Pierre de. *The Sacrament of the Present Moment.* Translated by Kitty Muggeridge. San Francisco: HarperSanFrancisco, 1989.

Francis de Sales. *Introduction to the Devout Life.* New York: Vintage, 2002.

Murray, Andrew. *Absolute Surrender.* Scotland: Eremitical, 1897, 2009.

Tozer, A. W. *The Pursuit of God.* Camp Hill, Penn.: Christian Publications, 1993.

Chapter 12: Lost in God's Love

Curtis, Brent, and John Eldredge. *The Sacred Romance: Drawing Closer to the Heart of God.* Nashville: Thomas Nelson, 1997.

McGinn, Bernard, ed. *Meister Eckhart and the Beguine Mystics: Hadewijch of Braband, Mechthild of Magdeburg, and Marguerite Porete.* New York: Continuum, 1994.

Miller, Calvin. *Into the Depths of God: Where Eyes See the Invisible, Ears Hear the Inaudible, and Minds Conceive the Inconceivable.* Minneapolis: Bethany House, 2000.

Phillips, J. B. *Your God Is Too Small.* New York: Macmillan, 1952.

Pink, Arthur W. *Spiritual Union and Communion.* Grand Rapids: Baker, 1971.

Tozer, A. W. *The Knowledge of the Holy.* San Francisco: HarperSanFrancisco, 1961.

*f*ormatio

TRADITION. EXPERIENCE.
TRANSFORMATION.

Formatio books from InterVarsity Press follow the rich tradition of the church in the journey of spiritual formation. These books are not merely about being informed, but about being transformed by Christ and conformed to his image. Formatio stands in InterVarsity Press's evangelical publishing tradition by integrating God's Word with spiritual practice and by prompting readers to move from inward change to outward witness. InterVarsity Press uses the chambered nautilus for Formatio, a symbol of spiritual formation because of its continual spiral journey outward as it moves from its center. We believe that each of us is made with a deep desire to be in God's presence. Formatio books help us to fulfill our deepest desires and to become our true selves in light of God's grace.